Symbols in
GAME OF THRONES

Other Works by Valerie Estelle Frankel

Symbols in GAME OF THRONES

The Deeper Meanings of Animals, Colors, Seasons, Food, and Much More

Valerie Estelle Frankel

With thanks to so many friends for so many *Game of Thrones* arguments, gushes, and discussions. You know who you are.

Contents

INTRODUCTION

When asked whether people should analyze his writing, George R.R. Martin, author of *A Game of Thrones*, replied:

> I think every writer appreciates attentive reading of his work. We labor over these books for years, after all. Then they come out, and the readers gulp them down in days or even hours. Which is very gratifying, in one sense, but can also be frustrating, if we feel that they are missing all the grace notes and little subtleties and clever allusions and ironies and turns of phrase that we sweated blood over for so long. I try to write books that will stand up to rereading, so that every time you go through you will find more to appreciate ... and therefore I'm thrilled when readers tell me that they do reread the books. ("So Spake Martin, C90, P15)

In fact, his series contains many clever homages, as well as items with deeper meaning. In a King's Landing puppet show, the Lion of Lannister defeats the Stag of Baratheon, while the Dragon of House Targaryen is returning to consume that lion. The Dothraki consider their horses part of themselves, Varys is a spider, the list goes on and on. With dogs, wolves, ravens, blood flies, and so many more, animal symbolism is endlessly significant.

Cersei loves to eat boar after one kills King Robert ... just as in Celtic myth, boars frequently heralded the deaths of noble warriors. Martin's ravens are straight from Norse myth, as are Krakens. Daenerys seeks to establish herself as good queen of Slaver's Bay, even while destroying their harpy that depicts the feminine as evil.

The animals of heraldry have much meaning when viewed through a medieval lens. It was the Normans who formalized heraldry and by the twelfth century many Norman lords had a "recognized" coat of arms. In heraldry, the horse is "a symbol of speed, intelligence and masculinity," much like Drogo the khal (Mounet Lipp). The Tully Trout are loyalty and prosperity; Baratheon antlers represent strength and fortitude.

Martin's endless banquets brim with symbolism as well. Popular dishes include "bloody beef," "blood sausages," "blood melons," "blood oranges," red wine, pomegranates, blackberries, cherries, grapes, and beets, underscoring the dripping red violence of the series. Characters to be sacrificed eat lambs, rich parasites eat lamprey, Arya catches pigeons as she adapts to an urban life in the slums of King's Landing. Frightening things are hidden in pies, and those characters covering fish in a thick crust or sauce are just as quick to hide their intentions. Daenerys tries hopelessly to plant olive trees in Meereen as the violence there escalates. "Every dish seems to have a double meaning. And some feasts appear to have one purpose but reveal much darker motivations that often end in disaster and death" (Kistler 133).

Seasons too have deeper meanings. There's the red comet that heralds war, violence, and dragons, with a different meaning for each character. Characters progress from being youths and the untried "knights of summer" through the tragedies of autumn and doom of winter to, one hopes, the resurrection of spring. The War for the Dawn is coming, as are the Rains of Castamere.

Colors have a section as well, from the blue of Daenerys's dress, casting her as the Virgin Mary, to the Black Brothers and White Cloaks. In heraldry, red represents martyrdom and a warrior's courage, while gold "signifies glory, faith, constancy, and wisdom" (Shepherd 343). Jojen Reed has the greensight, an ancient power of nature and the Old Gods. Ser Barristan and Brienne serve the realm humbly, as shown by their colors. Of course, there are the symbols of ice and fire: Stark children with red hair and blue eyes or swords of red and grey. Chief among these are the weirwood trees, red and white above black pools, with black ravens in their branches.

There are many more intriguing symbols, of course, as Daenerys's prophecies and protectors come in threes just like a fairytale. There are towers and water gardens, pyramids and the infamous Iron Throne.

As this book is designed for fans of books or show, it doesn't spoil major events from the books. This is the perfect guide for any fan of the series, especially one seeking deeper insights in the game and its players.

SYMBOLS IN GAME OF THRONES

ANIMALS

Bat

In the books, Jaime, then Brienne, wears the shield of the Black Bat of Lothar, accursed "arms of ill repute" from a house of Harrenhal that died out (IV.131). In fact, the bat symbolizes death and rebirth, as it emerges from caves in the womb of the earth each night. It can also suggest illusion, emphasizing Jaime and Brienne's desires to hide, remake themselves, and escape the burdens of past and family.

Bear

A black bear in a green wood is the sigil of House Mormont, vassals of House Stark. When Jeor Mormont "the Old Bear" took the black, he eventually became Lord Commander of the Night's

Watch. He holds the Mormont ancestral sword Longclaw, which he gives to Jon, remarking that wolves have claws as well as bears.

Jorah, Lord Jeor's son, is exiled by Ned Stark for selling slaves. He eventually pledges fealty to Viserys, then Daenerys. With her brother on the Wall and his son in exile, Maege assumes control of her House in the book. She and her warrior daughters are trusted warriors in King Robb's entourage, until the Red Wedding. As Commander Mormont describes her to Jon Snow:

> You are not the only one touched by this war. Like as not, my sister is marching in your brother's host, her and those daughters of hers, dressed in men's mail. Maege is a hoary old snark, stubborn, short-tempered, and willful. Truth be told, I can hardly stand to be around the wretched woman, but that does not mean my love for her is any less than the love you bear your half-sisters. (I.783)

The Lords of Bear Island are surrounded by legends that they can shapeshift into bear form, as the Starks can with wolves. Dacey describes a carving over her gates of "a woman in a bearskin, with a child in one arm suckling at her breast. In the other hand she holds a battleax" (III.630).

Myths speak of many shapeshifting bears, as they were considered one of the species closest to humans. The song "The Bear and Maiden Fair," popular at every celebration in Westeros, appears to be a Beauty and the Beast style story of the lovely maiden charming the savage creature. Like wolves, bears resemble humans in their intelligence and social interactions. They spoke to the basic, primitive side of mankind, as both Mormonts teach Jon and Dany practicality.

In heraldry, a bear is a symbol of healing and personal health and bravery (Mounet Lipp). He brings strength, cunning and ferocity to the protection of his clan. Thus Daenerys often calls large, hairy Jorah her "bear" in the books. She thought of her childhood protector, Ser Willem Darry, as a "bear" as well (I.31).

Other bears feature in the series, as Brienne must face a bear with a tourney sword in the third book or "The Bear and Maiden Fair." Bears are savage, wild creatures of course, especially those goaded by man. By defeating the creature, Jaime and Brienne cast themselves as a "bear and maiden fair" though neither resembles the label. In fact, they use quick-wittedness to escape, emphasizing that they must abandon their accepted roles and find new paths. There's a dancing bear at Joffrey's wedding and elsewhere, but these tend to be sad, awkward and elderly rather than dangerous, a reflection of nature's decline.

Birds

Varys is known for his "little birds" – small children from the Free Cities who spy for him. The Hound and Cersei call Sansa "little bird" on occasion. In the early seasons, Cersei's gowns are embroidered with birds, though she eventually develops a more ferocious motif. Costume designer Michele Clapton comments, "The bird embroidered on her clothes gives way to more and more lions" (Cogman 81).

Sparrows, religious followers named for the least assuming of birds, appear in the fourth book, bringing the dead to King's Landing to appeal for an end to war. "As the sparrow is the humblest and most common of the birds, they are the humblest and most common of men" (IV.420). They're "filthy, unkempt creatures, with leather shields and axes" (IV.357). While they seem harmless, they swarm the capitol in greater and greater numbers.

In each case, the bird imagery is meant to suggest a harmless, sweet quality, but the characters reveal themselves as far stronger than others assume. The sparrows of King's Landing, like lovely Cersei, unassuming Varys, and even little Sansa, all have a hard edge. Margaery laments that Joffrey's taste in necklaces probably runs to "severed sparrow heads," but he should not discount those weaker than himself ("Two Swords").

Daario, the pretty popinjay sellsword who joins Daenerys's crew, tells the others: "When you hear a songbird's whistle, you come. I'm a great whistler. The greatest in the land" ("The Rains of Castamere"). Though he appears pretty and useless, he's also a fearsome fighter.

Varamyr the skinchanger explains in the *A Dance with Dragons* prologue, "Bears, boars, badgers, weasels ... Haggon did not hold with such. Some skins you never want to wear, boy. You won't like what you become. Birds were the worst, to hear tell of it" (V.10). Birds don't symbolize freedom in the series, but a harmless appearance that soon turns deadly. The symbolism links up well here.

Cats

In heraldry, a cat is a symbol of liberty, vigilance and courage (Mounet Lipp). It is also a feminine icon, linked with the moon and various goddesses.

> The Roman goddess of Liberty was represented as
> holding a cup in one hand, a broken sceptre in the other,
> and a cat lying at her feet. No animal is so great an
> enemy to all constraint as a cat.
> The cat was held in veneration by the Egyptians as
> sacred to the goddess Bubastis. This deity is represented
> with a human body and a cat's head. Diodorus tells us
> that whoever killed a cat, even by accident, was by the
> Egyptians punished with death. (Vinycomb 207)

As Arya "chases cats" in the first book and season,
then strikes out on her own, she has a great deal of cat
symbolism herself. Arya is very adaptable. "From
working in the kitchens of Harrenhal to becoming 'Cat
of the Canals' in Braavos, she learns to accept her
situation for what it is and thereby to do what is
required" (Jacoby, "No One Dances the Water Dance"
242). In Braavos, "Cats liked the smell of Cat" and they
follow her about as she compares herself to the lean
scrawny ones (IV.510).

Catching cats indicates her increasing skill and
agility:

> Catching cats was hard. Her hands were covered with
> half-healed scratches, and both knees were scabbed
> over where she had scraped them raw in tumbles. At first
> even the cook's huge fat kitchen cat had been able to
> elude her, but Syrio had kept her at it day and night.
> When she'd run to him with her hands bleeding, he said,
> "So slow? Be quicker, girl. Your enemies will give you
> more than scratches." He had dapped her wounds with
> myrish fire, which burned so bad she had to bite her lip to
> keep from screaming. Then he sent her out after more
> cats. (I.338)

As she journeys the castle in search of them, she
also encounters one cat in particular:

> The Red Keep was full of cats: lazy old cats dozing in the

> sun, cold-eyed mousers twitching their tails, quick little
> kittens with claws like needles, ladies cats all combed
> and trusting, ragged shadows prowling the midden
> heaps. One by one Arya had chased them down and
> snatched them up and brought them proudly to Syrio
> Forel... all but this one, the one-eared black devil of a
> tomcat. "That's the real king of this castle right there,"
> one of the gold cloaks had told her. Older than sin and
> twice as mean. One time, the king was feasting the
> queen's father, and that black bastard hopped up on the
> table and snatched a roast quail right out of Lord Tywin's
> fingers. Robert laughed so hard he like to burst. "You
> stay away from that one, child" (I.338-339)

He becomes her nemesis in a way, but also her path to knowledge – she overhears Varys and Illyrio talking while on her quest to catch him. Thus the black cat functions as a replacement wolf in a sense, alerting her to unseen dangers and guiding her to a safe route from the castle.

Many fans wonder if he guarded another girl before Arya, or even functioned as her trusted warg companion. Varys comments:

> Rhaenys was a child too. Prince Rhaegar's daughter. a
> precious little thing, younger than your Arya. She had a
> small black kitten she called Balerion, did you know? I
> always wondered what happened to him. Rhaenys like to
> pretend he was the true Balerion, The Black Dread of old,
> but i imagine the Lannisters taught her the difference
> between a kitten and a dragon quick enough, the day
> they broke down her door. (I.636)

His name, for the great dragon of Aegon the Conqueror, speaks of strength as well as the human-animal bond. Many wonder if part of Rhaenys, Daenerys's niece, lives on in this black cat. When asked if he is Rhaenys' kitten, Martin replies only with an enigmatic "Could be." As the cat menaces Tommen's vulnerable black kittens – Ser Pounce, Lady Whiskers, and Boots – the ghost of the Targaryens seems to be haunting Tommen and preparing for his death, symbolically if not literally.

> From soup to sweet Tommen burbled about the exploits of his kittens, whilst feeding them morsels of pike off his own royal plate. "The bad cat was outside my window last night," he informed Kevan at one point, "but Ser Pounce hissed at him and he ran off across the roofs." (IV.276)

Many wonder at the significance of the large black tomcat as it prowls the palace and snarls at Tommen's beloved kittens. Does he represent the violence that will rebound from Rhaenys' death and kill Tommen? Does he represent catlike Arya, turned assassin and coming for the Lannisters? As a child, Joffrey cut open a pregnant cat and King Robert beat him severely for it. If cats in the castle are meant to be the sacrificed Targaryens, they're coming for Tommen with a vengeance.

Varamyr the skinchanger explains in the *A Dance with Dragons* prologue, "Cats were vain and cruel, always ready to turn on you" (V.10). In her later adventures, Arya is selfish and violent, training in feeling only callousness. One of her many personas is "Cat of the Canals," emphasizing her association with the wild creatures. She names herself, a sign of strength:

> She bit her lip. "Could I be Cat?"
> "Cat." He considered. "Yes. Braavos is full of cats. One more will not be noticed." (IV.326)

23

In a released chapter from *The Winds of Winter,* there's another link between cats and selfish violence: "Braavos was a good city for cats, and they roamed everywhere, especially at night. In the fog all cats are grey," Mercy thought. "In the fog all men are killers."

Lastly, Syrio tells Arya a story about a cat that seems to touch themes of the series. A Sealord tells everyone his cat is a magical creature, and all agree with him because he's rich and powerful, or they don't trust the evidence of their own eyes.

> "And to him I said, 'Each night in the alleys of Braavos I see a thousand like him,' and the Sealord laughed, and that day I was named the first sword."
> Arya screwed up her face. "I don't understand."
> Syrio clicked his teeth together. "The cat was an ordinary cat, no more. The others expected a fabulous beast, so that is what they saw. How large it was, they said. It was no larger than any other cat, only fat from indolence, for the Sealord fed it from his own table. What curious small ears, they said. Its ears had been chewed away in kitten fights. And it was plainly a tomcat, yet the Sealord said 'her,' and that is what the others saw. Are you hearing?"
> Arya thought about it. "You saw what was there."
> "Just so. Opening your eyes is all that is needing. The heart lies and the head plays tricks with us, but the eyes see true. Look with your eyes. Hear with your ears. Taste with your mouth. Smell with your nose. Feel with your skin. Then comes the thinking, afterward, and in that way knowing the truth." (I.531-532)

If Arya can learn this lesson, she will be a fierce warrior in truth.

Dragons

> He lifted his eyes and saw clear across the narrow sea, to the Free Cities and the green Dothraki sea and beyond, to Vaes Dothrak under its mountain, to the

> fabled lands of the Jade Sea, to Asshai by the Shadow,
> where dragons stirred beneath the sunrise. (I.136-137)

Bran's vision may indicate dragons still live in Asshai, or he may be seeing the past. Either way, dragons represent a world of magic and wonder, now returned along with the birth of Daenerys's trio. Pyat Pree tells her, "When your dragons were born, our magic was born again." As animal symbolism goes, dragons are far more powerful than lions, stags, or wolves – the mightiest of the mythic animals. He is also the bravest of all the creatures in heraldry (Mounet Lipp). In alchemy, dragons symbolize eternal change, a strong representation of Daenerys herself.

All cultures have dragons, and not just because of the prevalence of dinosaur bones. In humanity's cultural memory appears to be the giant lizard, fierce and terrifying.

> The ancients conceived it as the embodiment of malignant and destructive power, and with attributes of the most terrible kind. Classic story makes us acquainted with many dreadful monsters of the dragon kind, to which reference will afterwards be more particularly made.
> It is often argued that the monsters of tradition are but the personification of solar influences, storms, the desert wind, the great deeps, rivers inundating their banks, or other violent phenomena of nature, and so, no doubt, they are, and have been; but the strange fact remains that the same draconic form with slight modifications constantly appears as the type of the thing most dreaded, and instead of melting into an abstraction and dying out of view, it has remained from age to age, in form, distinctly a ferocious flying reptile, until in the opinion of many the tradition has been justified by prosaic science. It is surprising to find that the popular conception of the dragon – founded on tradition, passed on through hundreds of generations – not only retains its identity, but bears a startling resemblance to the original antediluvian

saurians, whose fossil remains now come to light through geological research, almost proving the marvellous power of tradition and the veracity of those who passed it on. (Vinycomb 59-60)

The word "dragon" comes from the ancient Greek for serpent. In Christian myth, it is often a force of evil, with the dragon being defeated by the heroic St. George, or Dracula taking his name from "dragon." Revelations 12:7-9 explains:

And there was war in Heaven: Michael and his Angels fought against the dragon; and the dragon fought and his Angels, and prevailed not; neither was their place found anymore in Heaven. And the great dragon was cast out, that old serpent, called the Devil, and Satan, which deceiveth the whole world: he was cast out into the earth, and his Angels were cast out with him.

St. George and the Dragon.

In variants of this image, a dragon can represent pure gluttony and avarice. In stories from the Norse Ring Saga to Narnia, terribly greedy characters slowly transform into dragons, and Smaug in *The Hobbit* is known for his hoard. Tyrion describes popular lore about dragons as "fodder for fools" including "talking dragons" and "dragons hoarding gold and gems," emphasizing that Martin's world uses dragons for another purpose (V:767).

This series abandons much of the evil and avaricious symbolism, in favor of the wonder and might of dragons. All bow before Daenerys when she hatches them, and rumors of her dragons spread around the world. Young Tyrion dreams of riding a dragon to feel the power and exhilaration of flight, far more magical than the wealth and privilege of the Lannisters.

People are also selfish to acquire dragons. They function in the center of the Westeros arms race – he who has dragons will win any battle. More importantly, they're a symbol of divine right and royalty in Westeros.

The Celtic dragon was an ancient symbol of fertility, wisdom, and immortality. This creature was worn on kings' torques as a sign of royal rule, then became a symbol of the York and Tudor kings of England. The Celts used the word "dragon" for "a chief," leading to legends of Arthur Pendragon. "Those knights who slew a chief in battle slew a dragon, and the military title soon got confounded with the fabulous monster" (Vinycomb 89). Today it's the Welsh dragon on the flag of Wales.

> Richard III as a badge had a black dragon. "The bages that he beryth by the Earldom of Wolsr (Ulster) ys a blacke dragon," derived through his mother from the De Burghs, Earls of Ulster... At the Battle of Bosworth Field Henry bore the dragon standard ... Henry VII., Henry VIII., Edward V., Mary and Elizabeth all carried the dragon as a supporter to the royal arms (Vinycomb 89)

Daenerys's Dragons

The three dragons hatched from Daenerys's eggs were given to her by Master Illyrio, who arranged her marriage in the first episode. She names them Viserion (white), Rhaegal (green) and Drogon (black, the largest and fiercest), after her two deceased brothers and her late husband, respectively. In Qarth, Daenerys is given a crown decorated with three dragons in those colors, a crown she wears through the books. As with the Starks and their wolves, the dragons express the emotions the diplomatic queen cannot. They frequently lash out at those she dislikes, especially Pyat Pree in Qarth and the slavers of Astapor and Yunkai. As Daenerys loses control of her dragons, her time in Meereen suggests losing control of herself and her purpose.

Historical Dragons

The three great dragons of Aegon the Conqueror and his sisters were Balerion, Meraxes, and Vhagar. Aegon rode Balerion, Rhaenys rode Meraxes, and Visenya rode Vhagar. Daenerys names her three ships for them after Qarth, emphasizing her kinship with the first conqueror. Aegon had two sister-wives, and Jorah tries to persuade Daenerys to have two husbands (one himself) to ride the dragons with her. Her ancestors never rode more than one chosen dragon, just as the Starks each have one chosen wolf.

Good Queen Alysanne, wife of Jaehaerys the Conciliator, rode a dragon named Silverwing. Balerion was killed some time in Jaehaerys's reign. Silverwing's fate is unclear.

Many dragons fittingly appear in the civil war called the Dance of the Dragons, shown in the novella, "The Princess and the Queen." Rhaenyra Targaryen, the queen apparent before her half-brother snatches the throne, rides the yellow dragon Syrax. "Syrax had long grown accustomed to chains; exceedingly well fed, she had not hunted for years" (749). Meleys, called the Red Queen, was an old she-dragon ridden by Princess Rhaenys Targaryen, Rhaenyra's aunt and mentor. "Her scales were scarlet and the membranes of her wings were pink. Her crest, horns, and claws were bright as copper. She had grown lazy but was fearsome when roused. Meleys was old, cunning and no stranger to battle" (713).

Rhaenyra's three oldest sons ride the bold young dragons Vermax, Arrax, and Tyraxes, all of whom die the same day as their riders. Her other son Aegon the Younger escapes capture riding his dragon Stormcloud for the first time, though the dragon dies just after. "The boy was white with terror, shaking like a leaf and stinking of piss. Only nine, he had never flown before ... and would never fly again" (730).

The princess's royal half-brother Aegon rides Sunfyre with gleaming gold scales and pale pink wing membranes. The Bronze Fury, Vermithor, is enormous and over a century old. Tessarion, the Blue Queen, dances with Seasmoke in the air, possibly in "more mating dance than battle" (773). She is Prince Daeron the Daring's, with "her wings as dark as cobalt and her claws and crest and belly scales as bright as beaten copper" (713).

Seasmoke is a pale silver-grey dragon of Dragonstone. Sheepstealer is a "notoriously ugly mud brown" (729). Grey Ghost is shy and pale in color. The Cannibal is "black as coal" and known for eating young dragons (779). All these are unclaimed dragons that Targaryen bastards attempt to ride during the war, with different levels of success.

Though the scent of the Targaryen bloodline helps, many dragons will eat frightened would-be riders instead of accepting servitude.

Targaryens

Dragons can also refer to the Targaryens, of course. Daenerys proclaims that her hero-brother Rhaegar was not the last dragon – she is.

> Ser Barristan: When your brother Rhaegar led his men at the battle of the Trident, men died for him because they believed in him. Because they loved him. I fought beside the last dragon that day, my grace. I bled beside him.
> Jorah: Rhaegar fought valiantly. Rhaegar fought nobly. And Rhaegar died.
> Daenerys: Did you know him well, Ser Barristan?
> Ser Barristan: I did, your grace. Finest man I ever met.
> Daenerys: I wish I had known him. But he was not the last dragon. ("Walk of Punishment")

When the children of the previous regime are killed, King Robert famously remarks, "I see no babes. Only dragonspawn" (I.112). Several Targaryens including Viserys proclaim they *are* the dragon or believe they can transform into one (thus one mad king drinks wildfire!). This may be more than madness, considering the Starks' warg power.

There's a vision in a released chapter of the sixth book:

> It was then that pasty, pudgy Teora raised her eyes from the creamcakes on her plate. "It is dragons."
> "Dragons?" said her mother. "Teora, don't be mad."
> "I'm not. They're coming."

30

> "How could you possibly know that?" her sister asked, with a note of scorn in her voice. "One of your little dreams?"
> Teora gave a tiny nod, chin trembling. "They were dancing. In my dream. And everywhere the dragons danced the people died."

Since only three (known) dragons remain in the world, it's likely dragons here means Targaryens and Targaryen claimants. Another civil war is coming, with the new kings Melisandre saw taking the old kings' places.

Other Possible Dragons

Dragon eggs are stored on Dragonstone Isle, home of dragonglass and many Targaryen secrets. The stone dragons around which the castle is built may in fact come to life as Daenerys's eggs do.

It's unclear whether the wolf Summer sees the red comet or something else when Bran and Rickon emerge from the Winterfell crypts in a type of rebirth: "The smoke and ash clouded his eyes, and in the sky he saw a great winged snake whose roar was a river of flame. He bared his teeth, but then the snake was gone. Behind the cliffs tall fires were eating up the stars" (II. 699). Did a dragon lie buried in the crypts under Winterfell?

Gold dragons are the most expensive currency, and characters sometimes make dragon puns. It seems unlikely that any prophecies about dragons battling or dragons coming forth from stone mean cold, hard cash, however.

There's also a constellation called the Ice Dragon. Martin wrote a short story about a living ice dragon, and many wonder if one dwells under the Wall. In *A*

Dance With Dragons, Jon repeatedly recalls Old Nan's tales of an Ice Dragon, which may prove significant.

Dragonflies

Dragonflies are magically glittering and lovely, but short-lived. The dress Joffrey has torn off Sansa is grey with dragonfly details, emphasizing Sansa's evanescent fragility. In Targaryen history, Duncan the "Prince of Dragonflies" appears to have died young while tragically in love with Jenny of Oldstones.

The dragonfly is a symbol of free will, apt for Prince Duncan who gave up his crown and married the woman he loved. Likewise in the short stories, Dunk admires dragonflies and daydreams about dragons when choosing to be an independent hedge knight. Sansa appears to have little free will, but slowly develops it as she learns to create her own destiny.

In Dany's last chapter of book five, "Insects buzzed around her, lazy dragonflies and glistening green wasps and stinging midges almost too small to see" (934). She is making a choice about a new destiny before her, as she seeks a world of permanence.

Eagle

"He can enter the minds of animals and see through their eyes." Mance Rayder says of the warg Orell in "Dark Wings, Dark Words." Orell in book and show is a wildling raider who can put his mind into the body of an eagle. This allows him to scout great distances. While Orell inhabits the eagle, Jon Snow kills his body, leaving the eagle with part of his personality. He flies at Jon and attacks him. This may all be foreshadowing if a Stark (or Snow) is killed and retreats into a wolf.

The eagle is generally a symbol of resurrection, as the eagle was believed to rejuvenate by flying into the sun. Psalm 103:5 explains, "Thy youth is renewed like the eagle's." Thus it makes a logical symbol for the warg who lives on in animal form.

Falcon

The falcon (indistinguishable from the hawk in heraldry) is the second most popular heraldic bird after the eagle. "Considering the very important past this bird played in the social life of earlier centuries, this cannot be a matter of any surprise" (Fox-Davies 181). The hawk is a masculine symbol of striving for great heights.

A white falcon on azure with the words "As High as Honor" is the sigil of House Arryn. The inaccessible height of the Eyrie helps to define it as the hawk's home. The hawk suggests swiftness and keen sight with great skill at the hunt – in fact, Jon Arryn unravels the mystery of Cersei's infidelity, though he isn't quite fast enough to reveal it before his death. In heraldry, the falcon or hawk is someone who eagerly pursues his goals and never rests until they're achieved...a mindset that sends Jon Arryn to his death (Mounet Lipp). The bird "may have been a medieval allegory of the evil mind of the sinner" (Cirlot 140). In fact Lysa Arryn hides many secrets.

The other notable hawk or falcon in the series is the one that killed the patriarch of Highgarden:

> Olenna: Do you know my son? The lord of Highgarden?
> Sansa: I haven't had the pleasure.
> Olenna: It's no great pleasure, believe me. Ponderous

33

oaf. My husband was an oaf as well, the late Lord Luthor.
He managed to ride off a cliff whilst hawking.
("Dark Wings Dark Words")

Again, the bird symbolizes male achievement and
lofty goals ... which in this case led to death. Like with
Jon Arryn, associating too much with the honorable,
powerful, and above all high-flying hawk becomes
fatal.

Goat

The goat is a symbol of practical wisdom in heraldry,
and an emblem of a man who wins through diplomacy
rather than strength of arms (Mounet Lipp). In
Christian symbolism, the goat is a devilish figure. It
represents fraud, lust, and cruelty, as well as the
damned at the Last Judgment. In the Renaissance the
goat usually appeared in art in order to distinguish
the sinners from the righteous. This interpretation is
based upon a Bible passage that relates how Christ
upon His coming shall separate the believing from the
unbelieving, as the shepherd separates the sheep
from the goats (Matthew 25:31-46).

Certainly Vargo Hoat, the "goat" of the books, is a
figure of vile cruelty, slicing off Jaime's hand to prove
his superiority. He wears a helm shaped as a goat's
head and his coat of arms feature the Black Goat of
Qohor, one of the faces of the Many-Faced God. Thus
the Brave Companions ride under the goat banner of
death.

While a prisoner of the Mountain, Wylis Manderly
was fed parts of the Goat while at Harrenhal.
Certainly, this stresses the Mountain's inhumane
treatment of prisoners under his protection. In fact,

it's Wylis Manderly's father who is treacherous, playing a deep game of politics with Davos, the Boltons, the Freys, the Lannisters, and the Starks.

Other goats appear alongside moments of fraud and treachery. Tyrion eats goat with Bronn just before revealing his past with Tysha, the wife Jaime and Tywin manipulated him into betraying. Ser Jorah orders a goat killed for Daenerys's supper upon hearing she's pregnant, then betrays her moments later by selling the news to King's Landing.

By contrast, Shagga of the Mountain Hill Clans is terribly violent, but not evil. He is loyal to Tyrion, despite his favorite tagline:

> Shagga: Shagga son of Dolf will chop off your manhood—
> Tyrion: —and feed it to the goats, yes. ("You Win or You Die")

> Tyrion: ...cut off his manhood, and feed it to the goats.
> Pycelle: Wha-no, no, no!
> Timett: There are no goats, halfman!
> Tyrion: Well, make do!
> Tyrion, Timett and Bronn snicker. ("What Is Dead May Never Die")

Griffon

House Connington of Griffin's Roost has arms of two griffins combatent on red and white. Jon Connington, a character of the fifth book, demonstrates a symbolic link with dragons as he sports his own magical creatures in colors of ice and fire.

The griffon, popular among the Babylonians, Assyrians, and Persians, has an eagle's head (or possibly lion's head) and eagle wings on a lion's body. A snake tail is included as well. They symbolize bravery, strength, alertness and endurance in the banners of heraldry (Mounet Lipp). "Griffons were considered to be good guardians: attentive, swift, brave, and tenacious" (Shepherd 229). Calling himself Griffon, Connington has indeed spent his life as a guardian. Both halves of the griffon creature "sacred to the sun," are positive, solar animals, thus the creature often represents salvation (Cirlot 133). It has yet to be seen if Griffon and his son Young Griffon will bring this to Westeros in the sixth book.

The mythic animal was popular in heraldry, possibly representing families in which an eagle and lion were united in marriage. It is unclear to what extent the ancients believed in griffons, and also whether they may appear in Westeros. Some beastiaries label the creature as clearly mythical:

> The griffin, gryfin, or gryphon, as it is variously termed by old writers, is best known as one of the chimerical monsters of heraldry – the mediæval representative of the ancient symbolic creature of Assyria and the East. It may be classed with the dragon, wyvern, phœnix, sphynx, "gorgons and
> hydras and chimeras dire," and other imaginary beings, that world of unreality grown up in the mind of man from the earliest times, the influence of whose terrors have exercised no little power in the progress of humanity. (Vinycomb 147-148).

Harpy

When Daenerys approaches Meereen, massive harpies support the city gates. The harpy is the symbol of Meereen and Old Ghis before it, the antithesis of all that is dragon and its ancient enemy.

In Greek myth, harpies ("snatchers") were horrible flying hags who tormented mankind. They lived in the world of the dead and had brass claws.

Though they don't appear in the heraldry of Westeros but in Old Ghis, they were in fact heraldic creatures.

> A poetical monstrosity of classical origin, described as "winged creatures having the head and breasts of a woman, and the body and limbs of a vulture; very fierce and loathsome, living in an atmosphere of filth and stench, and contaminating anything which they come near. Pale and emaciated, they were continually tormented with insatiable hunger." They are best known from the story of the Argonauts, where they appear as the tormentors of the blind king Phineus, whose table they robbed of its viands, which they either devoured or spoiled. They were regarded by the ancients as ministers of sudden death. (Vinycomb 179-180)

"They were portrayed as foul creatures, indicating a patriarchal priesthood taking over funerary rites" (Walker 258). The harpy represents all that is negative in the feminine, seen in male-controlled cultures like the Greeks, who described the vicious monsters tearing indiscriminately at noble heroes for imagined crimes. Daario comments, with his own touch of the patriarchy, "The harpy is a craven thing...She has a woman's heart and a chicken's legs" (III.774). Daenerys tears down the harpy throne in Meereen and appoints an ebony bench for herself, saying, "I will not sit in the harpy's lap" (III.980). She thus associates herself with being a good "mother" rather than a cruel hag, dragon rather than harpy. She refuses to be part of the harpy system: "In the afternoon a sculptor came, proposing to replace the head of the great bronze harpy in the Plaza of

Purification with one cast in Dany's image. She denied him with as much courtesy as she could muster" (V.43).

Horse

White horses in Norse folklore portend death in the family. Many mythologies use this image with death coming for people on a pale horse. A plague in the east becomes known as the "pale mare" and it does in fact bring death.

Aside from this, horse culture is found in the Dothraki, who eat horse meat, drink fermented mare's milk, make fires with dung, wear horsehair clothes, live in horsehair tents, and ride horses all their lives...and even after their deaths. The Dothraki city, Vaes Dothrak, features a great gate of bronze stallions. Horses often symbolize the power of mankind, as men domesticate the great animals and ride them. In heraldry "the horse is ready, ready for King and country. It is also a symbol of speed, intelligence and masculinity" (Mounet Lipp). They are often associated with the patriarchy, with straightforward conquests rather than subtle mysticism, much like the Dothraki themselves.

The great Dothraki prophecy features the Stallion Who Mounts the World. The ancient matriarchs of the city tell Daenerys:

> "As swift as the wind he rides, and behind him his khalasar covers the earth, men without number, with arakhs shining in their hands like blades of razor grass. Fierce as a storm this prince will be. His enemies will tremble before him, and their wives will weep tears of

blood and rend their flesh in grief. The bells in his hair will sing his coming, and the milk men in the stone tents will fear his name." The old woman trembled and looked at Daenerys almost as if she were afraid. "The prince is riding, and he shall be the stallion who mounts the world." (I.411)

This child dies before birth, and the prophecy may die with him. Of course, the prophecy of the "prince who was promised" is revealed by Maester Aemon to be gender neutral – Daenerys is the prince. She could potentially be this prince as well, and even lead a khalasar, or another army of "men without number" like the Unsullied. Her "children" the dragons could also fill this role, though much less literally.

Hound

"I like dogs better than knights. My father's father was kennelmaster at the Rock. One autumn year, Lord Tytos came between a lioness and her prey. Lioness didn't give a shit that she was Lannister's own sigil. Bitch tore into my lord's horse and would have done for my lord too, but my grandfather came up with the hounds. Three of his dogs died running her off. My grandfather lost a leg, so Lannister paid him for it with lands and a towerhouse, and took his son to squire. The three dogs on our banner are the three that died, in the yellow of autumn grass. A hound will die for you, but never lie to you. And he'll look you straight in the face." (Sandor Clegane, II.262)

Dogs appearing in heraldry were generally guard dogs – mastiffs or bloodhounds, greyhounds, foxhounds (Fox-Davies 154-155). The dog is the symbol for courage, vigilance and fidelity (Mounet Lipp). Joffrey's "Hound" fulfils a similar role, as he's appointed to the Kingsguard in season two.

Few actual dogs are seen in the series, and Sandor Clegane the "Hound" and his brother Gregor "the Mountain" are anything but tame. Nonetheless, dogs are generally thought of as man's partners, domesticated city creatures. Varamyr the skinchanger explains in the book five prologue,

> Dogs were the easiest beasts to bond with; they lived so close to men that they were almost human. Slipping into a dog's skin was like putting on an old boot, its leather softened by wear. As a boot was shaped to accept a foot, a dog was shaped to accept a collar, even a collar no human eye could see. (V.10)

In fact, the Mountain and the Hound both spend their lives dutifully serving the Lannisters, until Sandor is confronted with something he fears more – fire.

He runs from Blackwater and finds himself traveling with Arya in an attempt to ransom her. Though he claims to be working for himself, he goes to considerable effort to protect her ... he may have found himself a new master after all. After Arya gives up, he continues to push her. Arya thinks:

> If the Hound would have let her she would have sleep all day and all night. And dreamed. That was the best part the dreaming. If her nights were full of wolves, her day belonged to the Dog. Sandor Clegane made her get up every morning whether she wanted to or not. (III.883)

Gregor Clegane, the other brother with a three dog sigil, has "no splendor about him" with plain steel armor, dull gray and scarred with heavy use (I.685). Tyrion thinks of him as "an unthinking brute who led with his rage" (I.686). He is simple and loyal to the Lannisters, but a dog turned savage.

A few actual dogs appear in the series. Septon Meribald of book four has a pet called Dog, as he says the animal hasn't revealed his name yet. It protects him from wolves, and has killed a dozen. The Bastard of Bolton names his hunting dogs after his victims. Sansa finds a kinder pet:

> Sansa found Bryen's old blind dog in her little alcove beneath the steps, and lay down next to him. He woke and licked her face. "You sad old hound," she said, ruffling his fur.
> "Alayne." Her aunt's singer stood over her. "Sweet Alayne. I am Marillion. I saw you come in from the rain. The night is chill and wet. Let me warm you." The old dog raised his head and growled, but the singer gave him a cuff and sent him slinking off, whimpering. (III.940)

This dog is not only a protector but a substitute for Lady, though not a wholly effective one. His weakness emphasizes how much Sansa lacks in her real protector.

Insects

Drogo tells an enemy: "I will not have your body burned. I will not give you that honor. The beetles will feed on your eyes. The worms will crawl through your lungs. The rain will fall on your rotting skin until nothing is left of you but bones!" ("The Pointy End"). Thus here and elsewhere, insects are associated with vile decay and filth. After his injury, even before Daenerys's terrible bargain, he lies listlessly surrounded by bloodflies. Dany reflects on how ordinarily he hates them, but now he cannot be bothered to swat them away (I.702). The hatred of the bloodflies suggests a revulsion and fear at his own death, which in fact occurs far before he expects it.

Similarly, Meereen is full of flies. Daario notes, "Flies are the dead man's revenge. Corpses breed maggots and maggots breed flies" (III.981).

On the show, the Qartheen decorate their clothes with insects, suggesting a creepy-crawly association along with the glittering wings. Describing the costumes there, costume designer Michele Clapton explains, "It's so far removed from any place she's [Daenerys's] been before. We were able to take some risks with it" (Cogman 183).

Kraken

In a released book six chapter, Barristan asks his squire Tumco, whose young eyes can see more clearly, to identify the banners. Tumco says "Squids, big squids. Like in the Basilisk Isles, where sometimes they drag whole ships down." Barristan replies, "Where I'm from, we call them krakens."

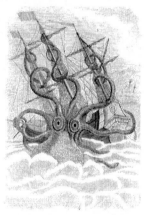

It appears krakens exist in truth in Westeros instead of just in mythology and heraldry. Varys reports an actual kraken attack off the Fingers, and more appear in an early chapter of book six, with krakens pulling down galleys after the blood rouses them. A battle with true krakens may be at hand.

The kraken is the sigil of the Greyjoys: The Red Priest Moqorro sees Theon's uncle Euron as "A tall and twisted thing with one black eye and ten long arms, sailing on a sea of blood" (V.447). There's a tentacle motif around Theon's father's keep.

In ancient myth, the kraken was a giant squid or leviathan, a great underwater beast that dragged ships to their doom. As it was ferocious and cruel but undetectable before it struck, it has clear symbolism with Theon Greyjoy as he turns on his allies and takes Winterfell. One bannerman comments, "You krakens have too many arms, you pull a man to pieces" (IV.27). Sea monsters symbolize "the unknown and mysterious abysses far from the sight of land" – the monstrous, savage sea itself (Walker 273).

Lion

"No figure plays such an important or such an extensive part in armory as the lion" (Fox-Davies 133). It is a symbol of majesty, courage and strength. "The lion has always enjoyed a high place in the heraldry as the emblem of undying courage, and hence that of a valiant warrior" (Mounet Lipp). The Lannister motto, "Hear Me Roar!" emphasizes this pride and power as their members play the game of thrones.

It is also a patriarchal symbol of proud men who need nothing from women – medieval bestiaries claimed lions were born dead until the father breathed on them and brought them to life. This is suitable for the family of Tywin and Jaime Lannister in which Cersei feels she cannot have a voice.

The lions of Lannister are often savage as well as majestic – Tywin wiped out House Castamere for its pride, as detailed in the popular Westerosi song, "The Rains of Castamere." Cersei's pride and rage can often be her undoing. Thus they share a lion's savagery and bloodthirstiness as well.

Mockingbird

Littlefinger made his own sigil, a silver mockingbird on green, with a pin to match. Mockingbirds certainly symbolize mockery, as their voices sound rude to observers. Littlefinger thus uses his position and outsider status to make cutting remarks and observations about the court. The birds symbolize a person who lacks individual expression, as they only taunt, rather than creating. While Varys claims he works for the good of the realm, Littlefinger appears only to please himself, committing murders to raise his own status. Seeing a mockingbird can indicate someone is committing adultery. Certainly, he tries to tempt Lysa and Catelyn, to say nothing of Sansa.

Ravens and Crows

It's said that dark wings bring dark words, an acknowledgement of ravens as unlucky birds. When asked why ravens are the designated messenger birds instead of pigeons, Martin responded:

> Ravens are smarter than pigeons, better flyers, more able to defend themselves against hawks and other predators, etc.
> I also liked the mythic resonances. Odin used ravens as his messengers, and they were also thought be able to fly between the worlds of the living and the dead.
> Would ravens actually be better carrier birds than

pigeons? Probably not... but it seemed to me that if I was going to have dragons and direwolves, that stretching the truth about ravens a bit was allowable as well. In the end, after all, A SONG OF ICE AND FIRE is a =fantasy= series. ("So Spake Martin" C90 P75)

Martin modeled his messenger ravens on Odin's, "able to fly between the worlds of the living and the dead" ("So Spake Martin," C90 P75). Odin, god king of Norse myth, was known for the two ravens, Hugin and Mugin (Thought and Memory), which sat on his shoulders and advised him, as the birds of the three-eyed crow do.

The legendary Targaryen bastard Bloodraven is so-named for his red raven-shaped birthmark, which proclaims his mystical destiny. He commanded a company of longbowmen called the Raven's Teeth in the Blackfyre rebellion century before.

In April 2013, Martin reported he was about a quarter of the way through *The Winds of Winter*, a few chapters of which he's read at conventions. Martin tells fans, "I have many many more pages to do, but I have some great stuff planned for it: a lot of blood and fire and death and devastation and ravens coming home to roost" (Prudom).

In the episode of Joffrey's wedding, Bran has a significant vision when he touches a Heart Tree: He sees the three-eyed crow that he's dreamed of since early episodes, followed by Ice in Ned's hands, Ned in the Black Cells, a man's voice telling Bran to "Look for me beneath the tree" and to go "North," a man's face within a tree, the female wight from the first episode, ravens, the White Walker's dead horse, the snowy and charred throne room of King's Landing from Daenerys's vision in the House of the Undying, Bran falling from the tower at Winterfell, and the shadow of a dragon over King's Landing.

What is the significance of Ned's appearance? Is the three-eyed crow offering to avenge Ned? Or is Ned's sword the crucial piece here? The three-eyed crow is in fact dwelling beneath the weirwoods and communicating through them, as suggested. The white walkers are coming, and a battle of ice, fire, and dragons may even reach King's Landing and destroy it unless Bran joins the battle.

Isaac Hempstead-Wright (Bran) comments, "I think the raven is a sort of a symbol of things to come for Bran—these sort of ancient powers that he's slowly learning how to use" (Cogman). Crows and ravens were symbolically identical (and indeed are related biologically). This emphasizes the Night's Watch, nicknamed crows for their black cloaks, are fabled defenders of prophecy as well. The three-eyed crow is an advisor for Bran, first in dreams and then in person. A third eye of course signifies higher wisdom. It gives him knowledge of past and future, though he lacks the training to understand:

> "I dreamed about the crow again last night. The one with three eyes. He flew into my bedchamber and told me to come with him, so I did. We went down to the crypts. Father was there, and we talked. He was sad."
> "And why was that?" Luwin peered through his tube.
> "It was something to do about Jon, I think." The dream had been deeply disturbing, more so than any of the other crow dreams. (I.611)

Crows in the western tradition are birds of ill-omen, war, and death, while in China they're a bird of prophecy. "The cawing of the black crow can be an omen of change" (Shepherd 202). Other significant crows of the series include Euron "Crow's Eye" Greyjoy and the mercenary group the Storm Crows, who may feature in prophecy as well. House Morrigen of Crow's Nest with a sigil of a black crow in flight on storm-green alludes to the dark war goddess and her link with crows and ravens.

In Celtic and Norse myth, the birds brought prophetic knowledge, but it was generally of violence, war, and trouble. The battle goddesses Badb (Crow) and the Morrigan (sometimes called *an badb catha,* or Battle Crow) took raven or crow form to bring dark omens (Davidson 87). Ravens could also be spirits of the dead returning. "King Arthur is thought by Cornishmen to have died and to have been changed into the form of a raven, and in medieval Wales souls of the wicked appear as ravens" (Henderson 360). In Celtic myth there's an even closer connection:

> The name Bran means crow or raven among the Celts. Crows were associated with the gods and prophecy, and sometimes were said to carry men's souls. They were also omens of war and death but would speak the truth to those wise enough to listen.
> In Celtic legend, King Bran (Blessed Raven) gave his sister Branwen away in marriage. However, in her distress, "she reared a starling in the cover of the kneading-trough, taught it to speak, and told it how to find her brother; and then she wrote a letter describing her sorrows and bound it to the bird's wing, and it flew to the island and alighted on Bran's shoulder" (Higgenson).
> Messenger birds are just as vital to Martin's series. Bran is not seen trying to rescue his sisters, but Jon is at one point.
> In battle to retrieve Branwen, King Bran was wounded in the foot with a poisoned dart. He bade his men to cut off and carry his head, which, still living, spoke and gave valuable guidance to his people. In his name, ravens are

> kept guarding the Tower of London, even today. Bran
> Stark too is crippled and must be carried, but he
> becomes a force of great wisdom, slowly reaching out to
> influence those he cares for. (Frankel, *Winning the Game
> of Thrones* 103-104)

Those who believe in the old ways are surrounded by ravens as well as Godswoods: Archmaester Marwyn, who believes in the Targaryens, lives in "the oldest building at the Citadel," the Ravenry, where flocks of ravens perch among an ancient but still-living Godswood (IV.680). The Blackwoods, possibly the only house in the Riverlands to still follow the old gods, have a sigil of a flock of ravens on scarlet surrounding a dead weirwood. A flock of ravens come to defend Sam and Gilly from the wights, "Shrieking, flapping, they descended on the wights in angry clouds" (III.647).

Mormont's raven deserves its own page because of the wisdom it brings Jon. While fans aren't completely certain, it's likely that the three-eyed crow or Bran himself (in the future) is sending messages through the bird, who otherwise only asks for corn. A few believe part of Mormont remains in the bird and is advising Jon, but events make that less likely.

Jon first notices Mormont's raven, when Mormont gives Jon a letter that says Bran is going to live. The raven repeats "Live!" even as the three-eyed crow begins sending Bran dreams of why he must come back. When Jon fights a wight, the raven shouts "Burn!" and Jon successfully burns the creature (I.567).

After Jon attempts to desert, Mormont asks whether Jon thinks Robb's war is more important than theirs. The raven flaps its wings and starts repeating "War." It also repeats the name of his lost uncle Benjen Stark (I.783). Of course, a vital war north of the Wall is coming. When Mormont suggests that Ned Stark himself sent Jon to the Wall, though nobody truly knows why, the raven repeats "Why?" (The simplest explanation for this last is that, as Ned says, Starks have considered it an honor to take the Black and have guarded the Wall for many generations. Perhaps they remembered Old Nan's wisdom better than those in the South.)

Jon later dreams he's defending the Wall from the Others, surrounded by people from his past. He wakes to find Mormont's raven pecking at his chest and calling him "Snow." After it says "king" (confirming for some that Jon is really a Targaryen, or possibly heir to the monstrous Night King who married a wight), the raven calls him by full name: Jon Snow. It seems to be warning him of upcoming danger. Time will tell who is warging inside the raven, though it could be multiple characters with conflicting agendas.

Sphinx

There are sphinxes at the gates of the Citadel, on the road in Old Volantis, and even in the Small Council chamber. They were a feminine symbol of the ancient mysteries, a multi-part animal mixed from lion and eagle, generally with a woman's head.

Maester Aemon, gravely ill, has delirious visions tinged with prophecy. He mumbles "the sphinx was the riddle, not the riddler." Alleras, known as the Sphinx, is a novice studying at the Citadel in Oldtown.

"He" appears to in truth be Sarella Sand, one of Oberyn Martell's bastard daughters who's "playing a game in Oldtown." A sphinx is the ultimate riddler and also the ultimate enigma. It is known for uniting disparate parts as well. It's clear that Alleras has more to offer than studying among men – she may be researching issues of succession, or the magic of ice and fire. Just as Dorne has played a long, subtle game, Alleras may be trusted to be doing so as well.

Spider

Varys is known for his secrets and plots, and thus called the "spider." The arachnid is known for sitting in its web, awaiting movement on the outskirts. Its destructive and stealth powers are also significant. "No matter how much the spider weaves, he is never loved," Varys says (III.1067). On the show, he adds, "No one weeps for spiders. Or whores" ("The Lion and the Rose"). In myth it can be a benevolent creature, known for hard work. Its constant weaving makes it a feminine symbol as it spins people's fates. At the same time, it's known for sitting in the center of bustle, patiently waiting like Varys himself. He's accused several times of being a poisoner like a spider, though he has many methods of disposing of his enemies.

Another spider, this time from the Dunk and Egg prequel stories, is called the Red Widow. She lost four husbands, whom she is rumored to have poisoned or killed by black magic. Lady Webber's sigil is a spider and her last name is suggestive as well. She combines the ruthlessness, poison, and feminine symbolism of her namesake.

Stag

The traditional sigil of House Baratheon is a black stag on a yellow field. Robert adds a crown and keeps it for his royal sigil. Stannis, follower of the Lord of Light, prefers a black stag encased within a red heart surrounded by yellow flames. Renly, allied with House Tyrell, merges their colors with his for a golden stag on a field of green. To the Celts, the stag was king of the forest and the key to the people's survival. The future ruler was the one who could slay the stag in the hunt.

Like the boar, the stag was an ancient Celtic symbol of sacrifice, as they would kill the stag as a substitute for the Horned God. Robert, Renly, and Joffrey, all stags, have untimely deaths as they're sacrificed for the realm like the ancient kings. The stag himself is "Wisdom, regeneration and growth, and virility. Because its antlers resemble branches, the Stag has been associated with the 'Tree of Life' and because of the way it renews its antlers, it is used as a symbol of regeneration" (Mounet Lipp). When one Baratheon dies, the next takes his place, and on, and on, through the series.

Joffrey wears a stag crown, as do Robert and Renly, signifying their Baratheon house. Of course, Robert and Renly are the first kings to die, suggesting the stag crown will be a faulty tool for winning Westeros. When the old stag dies in the first season, violence and chaos erupt across the realm. Of course, the stag is also an herbivore, a creature ill-equipped to battle lions and wolves. Varamyr the skinchanger explains in the ADWD Prologue, "Elk and deer were prey; wear their skins too long, and even the bravest men became a coward" (V.10). Tywin Lannister butchers a stag on his first appearance in season one, before the Lannisters do the same to the Baratheons.

In heraldry, antlers represent strength and fortitude (Mounet Lipp). Wildlings use antler cleats to climb the wall, especially on the show. Their garb mimics that of Inuit-inspired cultures, with leather and animal bones.

Trout

A silver trout leaping on a blue and red striped field is the sigil of Riverrun. A fish symbolizes many things, from plenty to sacrifice to fecundity, as mankind eats them to survive. Christ fed people infinite fish and loaves at a banquet. In heraldry, "fish are symbols of bravery and steadfastness. They are also symbols of economy, science, and symbols of the Christian faith. A fish constitutes a genuine, generous spirit" (Mounet Lipp).

"Because of the close relationship between the sea and the Magna Mater, some people have held fish to be sacred" (Cirlot 106). Catelyn, the epic story's mother, was born to the trout banner, and is called "a woman that was a fish" in a prophetic dream (III.249). Eating trout is taboo in a few Celtic legends. One tells of a beautiful white trout from the Otherworld; the man who kills it is cursed forever. The Freys presumably have a similar fate coming.

Tywin Lannister goes fishing in a cut scene from season three, emphasizing his predatory nature with the trout as his prey. Likewise, Joffrey serves trout to Sansa on the Kingsroad before he tempts her to betray her family. In King's Landing, they share another, this time baked in clay. Alan Kistler, author of *The Unofficial Game of Thrones Cookbook,* calls this a "fanciful" dish like Sansa's beloved ballads "but one that may foreshadow a future of captivity, not freedom" (146). Brienne actually dines on trout while seeking Sansa and thinking of the promise to her mother.

The Blackfish jokingly describes his house sigil during his videos on the Riverlands and House Tully.

> The trout, that most terrifying of fish, especially when it leaps out of the water. I suppose you don't have many [marriage] options when you live in the Riverlands. Our trout has swum up so many rivers over the centuries and leapt onto so many plates that it's a wonder that half the realm's sigils don't have fins by now.

Unicorn

Unicorns are famous through myth and heraldry. Though often believed to be sweet and gentle, their ferocious horn makes a powerful weapon. In Westeros, they are believed to live on the Isle of Skagos in the North. Several houses feature unicorns in their sigils, including Houses Brax, Wydman, Doggett, and Rogers.

Jon Snow, in a wolf dream, sees Rickon's Shaggydog battling a unicorn (most likely): "A wild rain lashed down upon his black brother as he tore at the flesh of an enormous goat, washing the blood from his side where the goat's long horn had raked him" (V.46). A unicorn symbolizes purity, harmony, and the arrival of spring. Rickon Stark's return from Skagos may bring all that to the Stark lands.

Viper

Prince Oberyn of Dorne is known as the Red Viper for the many poisons he uses. It's well known that anyone he scratches with his weapons will die. His brother Prince Doran explains:

> "Oberyn was ever the viper. Deadly, dangerous, unpredictable. No man dared tread on him. I was the grass. Pleasant, complaisant, sweet-smelling, swaying with every breeze. Who fears to walk upon the grass? But it is the grass that hides the viper from his enemies and shelters him until he strikes. Your father and I worked more closely than you know…" (V.510)

Inviting a viper into the community signifies cunning betrayal, and certainly, Oberyn craves vengeance against his Lannister hosts. The snake often represents a circle – the Lannisters and their favorite knight killed Elia of Dorne a generation before, and now Oberyn means to turn the tables on them. There are unsubstantiated fan theories that he may have actually poisoned Tywin Lannister with a slow-acting venom during his visit. In a book six scene, Martin summarizes Oberyn's origins, particularly his nickname:

> In his youth her uncle Oberyn had fought a duel with Edgar, had given him a wound that mortified and killed him. Afterward men called him 'the Red Viper,' and spoke of poison on his blade. The Yronwoods were an ancient house, proud and powerful. Before the coming of the Rhoynar they had been kings over half of Dorne, with domains that dwarfed those of House Martell. Blood feud and rebellion would surely have followed Lord Edgar's death, had not her father acted at once. The Red Viper went to Oldtown, thence across to the narrow sea to Lys, though none dared call it exile. And in due time, Quentyn

> was given to Lord Anders to foster as a sign of trust.
> That helped to heal the breach between Sunspear and
> the Yronwoods, but it had opened new ones between
> Quentyn and the Sand Snakes and Arianne had always
> been closer to her cousins than to her distant brother.

Snakes were symbols of the mother goddess long ago. While framed as evil in Judeo-Christian lore, snakes in ancient myths guarded treasures and sacred places, offered prophecies, and created new worlds. Oberyn's many illegitimate daughters, the Sand Snakes, are each lethal in different ways, but the deaths they crave could create a new regime. By the end of the saga, they may prove themselves all these symbols.

Wolves

Varamyr the skinchanger explains:

> A man might befriend a wolf,
> even break a wolf, but no
> man could truly tame a
> wolf. Wolves and women
> wed for life, Haggon often said. You take one, that's a
> marriage. The wolf is part of you from that day on, and
> you're part of him. Both of you will change. (V.10)

Certainly, the Stark children are not partnering with other animal companions. Each of them considers their wolf a best friend and mystic defender. The wolf signifies valor and guardianship, though wolves were also considered cruel and merciless (Mounet Lipp). Though they're less present on the show for reasons of budget, the book wolves are constant companions of Bran, Rickon, Jon, and Robb. They are very much the genesis of the story as well as its heart. Martin tells his fans:

> The first scene that came to me was chapter one of the first book, the chapter where they find the direwolf pups. That just came to me out of nowhere. I was actually at work on a different novel, and suddenly I saw that scene. It didn't belong in the novel I was writing, but it came to me so vividly that I had to sit down and write it, and by the time I did, it led to a second chapter, and the second chapter was the Catelyn chapter where Ned has just come back and she gets the message that the king [or rather, Jon Arryn] is dead. (*Vanity Fair*)

Jon is the one to notice the wolves' significance, as the first direwolf in generations travels down from the magical North and is killed by a stag: "Lord Stark. There are five pups. One for each of the Stark children. The Dire Wolf is the sigil of your house. They were meant to have them" ("Winter is Coming"). The pups are an omen, and in fact, House Baratheon, whose symbol is the stag, brings about Ned Stark's downfall by the end of the first season. Theon offers to kill the pups, a moment that also foreshadows his betrayal. Martin comments:

> All of the Stark kids have certain links to the wolf. I think in Westeros there's a certain amount of identification of all of these great houses to their sigils, to the animal charges that they bear. The Lannisters are always likening themselves to lions, for example, and their motto "Hear me roar" speaks of a certain way of looking at life. But I think for the Starks it goes a little bit beyond that, especially in this generation, with these direwolves. It's more than just a handy metaphor with them. (Shaw)

These are not traditional wolves, but larger, fiercer direwolves. Martin explains:

> Direwolves were an actual species of prehistoric wolf.
> They have long been extinct, of course, so there is much
> we can't know about them... but I have used much of
> what we =do= know for my own direwolves. Of course, I
> have also claimed a fantasist's prerogative to make
> everything bigger and more spectacular. Direwolves were
> larger than modern wolves, but not as large as my
> versions. ("So Spake Martin" C91 P105)

Ned calls Arya's wildness "the wolf blood" (I.221), and warns her, "When the snows fall and the white winds blow, the lone wolf dies but the pack survives" (I.222). In fact, the Starks are soon torn apart, and their wolves as well.

Each wolf echoes more than its owner's power and lifeforce – it's their hidden impulses, desires and wishes. As such, the wolves are the unconscious shadows of their owners, enacting the fear and rage or hidden sensitivity that exists beneath the rational mind. The wolves lash out in fear or anger, while their humans are forced to be polite and civilized. Of course, the wolves' warnings are always accurate, and the children ignore them at their peril.

Ghost

Jon Snow is the one to observe there is the right number of pups for the legitimate Stark children. His own tiny albino runt is lying hidden in the snow, part of his wolf pack but separate, as Jon is from the Starks. Ghost's presence also confirms that Jon is a Stark like the other children and heir to a similar magic.

> Shaw: At one point Greywind characterizes Ghost as the
> quiet one who was "one of them but not one of them."
> Since the direwolves seem to reflect the children, does
> this characterization of Ghost mean that Jon is somehow

a part of but still separate from the people around him?
Martin: Oh yes, I think that's always been true. Even in
Winterfell, as a kid before the wolves, Jon was the
bastard. He was the odd one out. The rest of them are all
brothers and sisters. He's only a half-brother, so he's not
as closely tied to them. In some circumstances he could
share everything with his brothers, he could train with
Robb and all that, but then another circumstance would
come up (like when the king came to the castle and they
were choosing who could sit at the high table) and he's
not welcome there. So he's of them, he's part of the
family, he's part of the siblings, but he's a little bit apart
too. Ghost is very similar to that. He's the albino, he's the
one who makes no noise, so he's related to the other
direwolves but one apart as well. (Shaw)

At the outset, Ghost is the unwanted runt of his pack,
but he grows to be the largest, suggesting a mighty
destiny for Jon. Jon names him for his white fur and
silence, but the name also evokes a connection with
death and the mystical.

Martin notes, "There is a significant point, though,
concerning Jon and Ghost in the third novel. There is a
period in the novel where he cannot feel him, he
cannot sense him as he previously did, then he can
again. That's a minor but still significant plot
point" (Shaw). This occurs when Jon cannot bring
Ghost over the Wall, so he must order him away.
Later, Jon can't feel Summer when Bran goes beyond
the Wall ... was Ghost visiting shapechangers,
Children of the Wood, or Others?

Like the other wolves, Ghost offers warnings and
acts on Jon's buried desires. When Jon deserts
the Night's Watch, Ghost betrays their position so that
Jon's friends can bring him back. (Is this Jon wishing
on some level to keep his oath, or is this the three-
eyed crow and the old gods, knowing that he'll be

needed up North?) Ghost is likewise the one to discover the cache of dragonglass weapons near the Fist of the First Men. Jon sometimes rides in Ghost's mind in his dreams, though he doesn't fully understand what's happening.

Grey Wind

When Greatjon Umber menaces Robb during an audience, Grey Wind eats two of his fingers. The Greatjon acknowledges with a laugh, "Your meat is bloody tough!" and pledges his support ("The Pointy End"). During the War of the Five Kings, the "Young Wolf" is best known for Grey Wind, who battles by his side.

> Arya: They call him the young wolf. They say he rides into battle on the back of a giant direwolf. They say he can turn into a wolf himself when he wants. They say he can't be killed.
> Tywin: [smiling] And do you believe them?
> Arya: No, my Lord. [staring right at him]. Anyone can be killed.
> ("The Ghost of Harrenhal")

Grey Wind does not like the smell of some of the relatives of Robb's wife (a Westerling sworn to House Lannister in the books), and Catelyn fears a treachery that soon occurs. She tells Robb, "Any man Grey Wind mislikes is a man I do not want close to you. These wolves are more than wolves, Robb. You must know that. I think perhaps the gods sent them to us. Your father's gods, the old gods of the north" (III.198). Just before the Red Wedding, Grey Wind growls at and attacks the Freys, so Robb has him confined outside.

Boy-king and wolf die at the same time, and the wolf's head is nailed onto Robb's shoulders in a cruel insult.

Lady

Lady is the smallest of the wolves, symbolically the most vulnerable. Cersei orders her killed from sheer spite, because she cannot punish Arya or Arya's wolf for hurting Joffrey. Thus Lady dies, by the hand of Ned Stark. He says, "The wolf is of the North. She deserves better than your butcher" and sends her to be buried at Winterfell ("The Kingsroad"). This mirrors Sansa's life in King's Landing – tormented by the Lannisters because of her family after Ned has endangered her by bringing her there. It's unclear whether Sansa will ever return home.

Unlike her siblings, Sansa reveals no prophetic dreams or wolf senses – Lady's death appears to have robbed her of her inner wildness and power forever. She also loses the supernatural sensitivity that warns her siblings of trouble. Sansa believes Lady could smell out falsehood (II.214) but with her dead, Sansa believes in the queen and Joffrey until it's too late. Several times in the third book, she wishes she had Lady to comfort her and make her feel brave, but she only has an old dog of Littlefinger's.

Nymeria

> Arya: Jon, watch this. Nymeria! Gloves!
> Nymeria: [Ignores her]
> Jon: ...impressive.
> Arya: Shut up. [Clears throat and speaks firmly and clearly] Nymeria! Gloves!
> Nymeria: [Tilts head and looks at Arya quizzically]
> Arya: ARGH! ("The Kingsroad")

Arya finds clever uses for her wolf earlier than her siblings do. Of course, Arya must chase her away after she savages the brutal Joffrey.

Nymeria is named for the warrior-queen who conquered Dorne with ten thousand ships, a reflection of who Arya wants to become (in contrast with Sansa's "lady"). In the forests, Nymeria grows fiercer and angrier, leading an army of wolves and savaging the soldiers that took Arya's family: "She has been known to bring down aurochs all by herself, that no trap or snare can hold her, that she fears neither steel nor fire, slays any wolf that tries to mount her, and devours no other flesh but man" (IV.373). As such, she appears to be Arya's wrath, wild and free in the wilderness. While Arya remains hidden, longing to join Robb and fight, Nymeria tears up the countryside and leads an army of wolves.

> The series' other monster of female rage is Nymeria, Arya's wolf. She represents Arya's fury and savagery, which Arya must chase away in order to conform to the Lannisters' rules and live in King's Landing. In the second book, Arya hears about an enormous female wolf who has risen to packleader and has no fear of men. In time, Nymeria leads hundreds of man-eating wolves and fills the forests with her rage. In Arya's dreams, she thinks, "Some of her little grey cousins were afraid of men, even dead men; but to her meat was meat and men were prey. She was the night wolf" (V.593). As a killer of knight and peasants alike, howling in the forest, Nymeria becomes the bane of society.
>
> Though the wolf hasn't yet impacted the plot, she remains at the edge of Arya's consciousness, like a sixth sense. Arya reflects to herself that she may "no one," but the names she repeats to herself are "the night wolf's prayer. Someday she will find them, smell their fear, taste their blood" (V.593). Nymeria is her seething magic, rage, and power, distant from her but still thriving. When Arya

returns to Westeros, Nymeria may do more to aid her.
(Frankel, *Women and Game of Thrones* 147)

Summer

After Bran's fall, Summer spends his time howling beneath his window. When an assassin comes, Summer kills him, defending Bran and Catelyn. Bran awakes from days of prophetic dreams and names his wolf Summer, his ally against the long winter he is chosen to combat.

Jojen Reed comments, "The black one [Rickon's wolf Shaggydog] is full of fear and rage, but the grey is strong ... stronger than he knows ... can you feel him, sister?" (II.333). On his travels, Bran sends Summer to aid Jon Snow. Beyond the Wall, Summer wins the wolfpack of another shapeshifter.

When Sam and Bran meet, Bran only agrees to follow him after Summer licks Sam's hand. Sam, frightened of nearly everything, is unafraid of Summer, remarking that he knows Jon's Ghost well. As Summer defends Bran while Bran travels in his mind, he appears to be the gateway for Bran's prophetic dreams.

Shaggydog

Rickon behaves increasingly badly as his family, in his eyes, abandons him. When Bran dreams through Summer's eyes, he sees Shaggydog searching desperately for his mother and pack, as Rickon is doing while awake.

If Rickon is behaving badly, Shaggydog is behaving far worse, to the point of savagery. This reaches a climax when Rickon's father dies and he hides in the crypt. Shaggydog savages the Maester, and it's revealed that he's attacked two other men before this. Bran understands that the wolf "was not made for chains" (I.735) but both Rickon and Shaggydog are acting out of control. Shaggydog and Summer are confined to the godswood in the second book after Shaggy bites their untrustworthy ward, Little Walder Frey.

Shaggydog stays with Rickon on their quest North and protects Rickon as boy and dog set out alone with Osha. The other wolves dream of him and call him their savage brother.

SYMBOLS IN GAME OF THRONES

FOOD

Apples

Littlefinger eats an apple and then throws it into the water before he offers to bring Ned to Catelyn in King's Landing. Jon eats a "small, withered apple" before deserting the Night's Watch (I.777). Cersei serves apples twice on the menu as she and her ladies await victory or death from Ser Ilyn during the Battle of Blackwater. For all these characters, choice, temptation, and worldly goals are paramount, as they eat apples while standing at a crossroads.

In Norse and Celtic mythology, apples were the fruit of the Gods, while in the Bible, they suggest temptation. In its roundness, the apple represents totality or worldly desires (Cirlot 14). Thus a desire for the riches of the world led to original sin. A golden apple and the choice of which goddess deserved it began the Trojan War. In each case, the apples brings godlike knowledge and power, but with it, a capacity to be destroyed.

Jaqen H'ghar casually munches an apple on the show after killing a man for Arya. She has two remaining to choose. Likewise, Theon freezes, still chewing on his apple when Osha takes off her clothes in front of him and offers him an alliance in "The Old Gods and the New." He accepts, and she betrays him. Tyrion's favorite red leather jerkin has snakes and fruit decorating it as well as lions, linking him with the choices of Eden.

The Riverlands team with apple trees. Arya, Hot Pie, and Gendry encounter dead men hanging from apple trees after they escape Harrenhal, and villagers give dried apples to the Brotherhood Without Banners. Arya thinks of her list and remembers Jaqen's offer before she eats a wormy apple herself. She throws crabapples at Gendry when torn between conflicting futures. In the fifth book, Jaime comments that scouts have found men in the Riverlands hanged on crabapple trees with crabapples trapped in their mouths. The Brotherhood Without Banners and their infamous lady appear to be taking a godlike revenge against all who prey on the innocent, as they also emphasize the brutal choices their victims once made. Jaime eats a meal with dried apples before Brienne leads him to Lady Stoneheart in the fifth book. This time the fateful choice is hers.

Tommen adores applecakes, though admittedly, he's too young to make the hard decisions ... at least, so far. Similarly, Alan Kistler, author of *The Unofficial Game of Thrones Cookbook*, comments, "Little Rickon is too young to do much more than follow his would-be saviors or captors – or worse. He enjoys an apple cake while others plan his future for him" (Kistler 199). Soon, others will be making hard choices on whether these boys will live or die, rule or be supplanted. While Sansa has few significant apple moments, it should be noted that there is a variety of apple called a "sansa" – she may have to make this greatest choice of all.

When Davos comes to White Harbor, he buys a dry, mealy apple from a vendor. "Davos felt a pang of guilt. They came here for refuge, to a city untouched by the fighting, and here I turn up to drag them back into the war. He took a bite of the apple and felt guilty about that as well" (V.196). He and Lord Manderly both find themselves at significant crossroads.

As Jon makes clear in the fifth book, an apple can mean a major choice one can take the safe path or the dangerous, fight temptation or succumb to it, choose worldly wealth or honor.

> The black brothers began to pass out food. They'd brought slabs of hard salt beef, dried cod, dried beans, turnips, carrots, sacks of barley meal and wheaten flour, pickled eggs, barrels of onions and apples. "You can have an onion or an apple," Jon heard Hairy Hal tell one woman, "but not both. You got to pick." [...]
> "Hal, what was it that you told this woman?"
> Hal looked confused. "About the food, you mean? An apple or an onion? that's all I said. They got to pick."
> "You have to pick," Jon Snow repeated. "All of you. [...] those who want to help us hold the Wall, return to Castle Black with me and I'll see you armed and fed. The rest of you, get your turnips and your onions and crawl back inside your holes." (V.273-274)

Arbor Gold

This pale wine is richly prized in Westeros and beyond, but usually represents treachery and lies when served. In *A Feast for Crows*, Littlefinger describes his negotiating with the Vale lords as serving up "lies and Arbor gold" (IV.147). When he tells Sansa all the lies she must tell to keep safe, he serves her more of the same: "The wine was very fine; an Arbor vintage, she thought. It tasted of oak and fruit and hot summer nights, the flavors blossoming in her mouth like flowers opening to the sun. She only prayed that she could keep it down" (III.931). Much like the lies, it's hard to digest.

When Manderly serves disturbing pies to the Freys, who killed his son at the Red Wedding, he smilingly tells them, "Wash it down with Arbor gold and savor every bite. I know I shall" (V.493). There's also an Arbor gold poisoning in "The Princess and the Queen" as Ser Hobart Hightower brings his enemy the gift of a cask, then is forced to share it. "Rather than betray his fellow Caltrops, he let the squire fill his cup, drank deep, and asked for more" (775). Soon enough, both men are dead. Finally, it's rumored that a courtier may have saved a Targaryen baby, swapping him with a tanner's son for a jug of Arbor

Gold. Wherever the wine appears, treachery and lies accompany it.

Beets and Turnips

Bran offers beets to Little Walder Frey and turnips to Big Walder Frey at the Winterfell harvest feast, in contrast with the sweets he sends to people he loves. While this seems a small, childish gesture, it must be remarked that beets are the color of blood and turnips have a sour taste. Cold turnips and beet salad are on the menu at the Red Wedding.

Jon's friend Pyp reverses Melisandre's doom-riddled words with a slogan of his own: "The night is dark and full of turnips. Let us pray for venison, my children, with some onions and a bit of tasty gravy" (V.144). His version, of course, is innocent and bloodless.

At the beginning of book four, Cersei and her uncle Kevan eat beets after a significant death. Beets are also part of the meal she eats with Balman and Falyse (when Cersei thinks how much she's come to love boar and plots more deaths). As she embarks on political manipulations, her hands are covered with red juice. Meanwhile, Tommen wishes to outlaw beets – a sign of balking at his mother but also an indicator he's tired of the endless bloodshed.

In the East, Tyrion offers Penny a share of his buttered beets and apologizes for her brother's death. Quentyn eats syrupy beet soup in Volantis, where the Widow of the Waterfront says, "Should you reach your queen, give her a message from the slaves of Old Volantis...Tell her we are waiting. Tell her to come soon" (V.371). A slave uprising is brewing, and with it more violence.

Blackberries

Catelyn eats blackberry preserves just after washing off the blood of Bran's assassin. Lysa eats blackberries and cream at Tyrion's trial at the Eyrie:

> Pitchers of thick cream and baskets of blackberries had been set out, and the guests were sipping a sweet orange-scented wine from engraved silver cups. A fool's festival, Brynden had called it, and small wonder.
>
> Across the terrace, Lysa laughed gaily at some jest of Lord Hunter's, and nibbled a blackberry from the point of Ser Lyn Corbray's dagger. They were the suitors who stood highest in Lysa's favor ... today, at least. (I.434)

This purple fruit drips crimson juice, much like bloodstains. Thus Lysa celebrates the upcoming bloodshed she craves, as bloody juice runs down her chin from  a suitor's dagger. King Robert roars, "You smell like blackberry jam" to a prostitute on the show, hinting at the violence to come ("Cripples, Bastards, and Broken Things").

Also, blackberries can symbolize a trap: "Once caught in blackberry brambles – seemingly so innocent – their thorns will only dig deeper into the traveler who tries to press forward; the only way out is back" (Kistler 207). When Arya travels with Yoren, the children of the book pick blackberries several times. In fact, they're doomed to die in an upcoming slaughter. Likewise, Brienne and Jaime "broke their fast on oatcakes, salt fish, and some blackberries that

Ser Cleos had found, and were back in the saddle before the sun came up" (III.160). Soon enough, Ser Cleos will be slain, and the pair taken prisoner.

When Bran wargs, he's surrounded by the fruit, mashed into the earth: "The evening's rain had woken a hundred sleeping smells and made them ripe and strong again. Grass and thorns, blackberries broken on the ground, mud, worms, rotting leaves, a rat creeping through the bush" (II.663). The Liddle who encounters Bran and his friends on the road gives them oatcakes with pinenuts and blackberries in them. Bran soon faces his first battle on the road, when he sends Summer to rescue Jon Snow.

Renly serves Catelyn blackberry tarts before his murder. Illyrio and Tyrion have blackberry wine and "Illyrio offered him a bowl of blackberries in cream" as they plot a war. Tyrion waves the latter away – he has had enough of war and violence (V.76).

Queen Talisa notes of Catelyn, "If she had her way, I would be back in Volantis playing my harp and you would be sitting over there eating blackberries out of Roslin Frey's hand" ("The Rains of Castamere"). The blackberries stain Edmure and Roslin with red juice, moments before the violence of the Red Wedding. Before Joffrey's wedding, similarly, "They broke their fast on honeycakes baked with blackberries and nuts" (III.802). Weddings are a bloody business in Westeros.

Blood Oranges

When Sansa says that Mycah attacked Joffrey, Arya squeezes her blood orange so that "red juice" flows from it, and then flings it at Sansa, staining her white gown from the queen (I.476). Thus she suggests that

Sansa is far from blameless in her friend's death. As "blood" stains the dress the queen gave her for her engagement, Sansa must reflect on what the betrothal has cost. She later dyes the gown black in mourning for King Robert and pleads for her father's life in it.

Oranges famously symbolize death in the *Godfather* films, and the wording of "blood oranges" is just as significant. As the Sand Snakes urge war, rotting blood oranges tumble down around Prince Doran of Dorne.

> "The blood oranges are well past ripe," the prince observed in a weary voice. "It is long past time for bloodshed." A few had fallen to burst open on the pale pink marble. The sharp sweet smell of them filled Hotah's nostrils each time he took a breath. No doubt the prince could smell them too. (IV.36)

The strong smell and pink marble also suggest spilled blood. He doesn't react when the first two fall near him, but at the third, he appears to wince in pain. Some compare these to his family deaths – the third will prove too much for him.

> He was still groping for some words to say when another orange fell with a heavy splat, no more than a foot from where the prince was seated. Doran winced at the sound, as if somehow it had hurt him. "Enough," he sighed, "it is enough. Leave me, Areo. Let me watch the children for a few more hours." (IV.36)

After whisking her from King's Landing, Littlefinger

serves Sansa fruit including "apples and pears and pomegranates, some sad-looking grapes, a huge blood orange" (III.933).

> Lord Petyr cut the blood orange in two with his dagger and offered half to Sansa. "The lads are far too treacherous to be part of any such scheme…and Osmund has become especially unreliable since he joined the Kingsguard. That white cloak does things to a man, I find. Even a man like him." He tilted his chin back and squeezed the blood orange, so the juice ran down into his mouth. "I love the juice but I loathe the sticky fingers," he complained, wiping his hands. "Clean hands, Sansa. Whatever you do, make certain your hands are clean." Sansa spooned up some juice from her own orange. (III.935)

Littlefinger metaphorically offers to share bloodshed with Sansa, though he advises her to keep her hands clean of it, and she literally does. By book's end, they have worked together – Littlefinger to murder someone, and Sansa to cover it up.

Lysa sips orange-scented wine as she forces Tyrion into trial by combat. The Kindly Man sweetens his breath with oranges and Septon Meribald passes out oranges on his journey through the Riverlands. While the Septon seems kind, he's also observing the war's effect on the commonfolk. The Fiddler, a rebel plotting against the throne in the short story "The Mystery Knight," smells of oranges, limes, and exotic spices (676). Admittedly "blood oranges" are not mentioned specifically in these instances, yet the linked association lingers.

Cersei and Tommen share breakfast of "some blood oranges newly come by ship from Dorne" in the fourth book. War is also coming from Dorne, and Cersei and Tommen's doom may come soon as well.

Boar

"I paid the bastard back, Ned. I drove my knife right through his brain ... I want the funeral feast to be the biggest the Kingdoms ever saw. And I want everyone to taste the boar that got me" ("You Win or You Die").

> Robert dies gored by a boar. The boar is often directly or indirectly involved in the death of the hero in the great myths and epics, from Culhwch and Olwen to Adonis. In Celtic tradition, the boar was associated with courage and strength as well as sovereignty and protection of the land. "The ancient Greeks associated the boar with winter, so its killing represented the slaying of winter by the solar power of spring" (Shepherd 182). By contrast, this boar kills the king, and with his death, summer changes to autumn, just as the kingdom deteriorates into war. The courage and strength has killed King Robert rather than allowing him to prevail.
>
> Likewise, the warrior Diarmuid stole away Grainne, his lord Fionn MacCumhail's betrothed. When he and the lady finally returned, Fionn and Diarmuid went on a hunt and Diarmuid was wounded by a giant boar. Fionn knew he could heal Diarmuid by letting him drink water from his cupped hands, but several times he let it spill through his fingers and Diarmuid died. From the affair to the betrayal and death of a warrior, Robert's death has parallels. (Frankel, *Winning the Game* 104)

It's fitting that King Robert is gored by a boar and dies of it. Symbolically, the boar is intrepid and carnal, like the king (Cirlot 30). The boar is the Celtic symbol of endurance and courage. Also, as seen above, many heroes and kings had such a death, linked with a new world and new regime. At the historical Black Dinner, on which the Red Wedding is somewhat based, the head of a black bull or boar was served.

Other boar appearances in the series have a similar meaning. King Robert is hunting boar while Bran is pushed out a window. After Yoren's death and just before their capture by the Lannisters, Arya and her friends discuss hunting boar. Boar is served at the Winterfell harvest feast before the Theon invades, and Bran gives the lord's portion to the "boisterous Umbers" (II.325). Cersei eats boar with the Merryweathers while scheming to bring down her enemies. Tyrion tells Jaime, "Try the boar. Cersei can't get enough of it since one killed Robert for her," and on the show, Cersei feels the same ("The Lion and the Rose").

After Robb beheads Rickard Karstark, Jeyne sends him boar for dinner and he refuses to eat it, trying to symbolically stave off the inevitable desertion by all of Rickard's forces. Many other boar appearances follow, all connected with a regime change – the death of the old king and arrival of the new:

> Roose wants boar after hunting wolves while he's at Harrenhal; the castle switches hands again soon, after both literally (Bloody Mummers) and on paper (Littlefinger gets it). This is also about the time that Roose's allegiances are switching or have switched. Sansa has boar with the Queen of Thorns, when the plot is on to assassinate Joffrey. Alerie offers boar to Sansa; the Tyrells are co-opting her. Boar is served at Joffrey's wedding. Cersei eats it with the Stokeworths when plotting against Bronn, only for Bronn to end up on top. Cersei, heh, comes to like boar. Ryman Frey uses boar-baiting to keep his men in line at Riverrun; he ends up getting hanged and popular assumption is that the Freys will lose Riverrun. On the way to the pit fight, a Brazen Beast in a boar helm offers Dany's litter carrier water. A boar gores Barsena in the fighting pit in Meereen before Dany flies off on Drogon and leaves a power vacuum behind. DP points out that the fighting pit chapter, which

ends in massive political upheaval, is rife with boars and boar symbolism. Borroq's boar gives Ghost (and Jon) fits on the Wall. Jon, however, tries to prevent Ghost from savaging the boar or fighting the boar. ("The Food Code of Ice and Fire")

Bread and Salt

Bread, the most basic food, has always been a symbol of sustaining life. In Westeros, it's puffy western bread, while in Essos and Dorne it's Mediterranean flatbread. Bread and salt represent an entire meal, all that is necessary for existence. Thus eating both asserts the relationship of guest and host has been offered and accepted: neither person can murder the other. In ancient times, with only public inns and private residences available for shelter, such laws had to be established to prevent utter chaos: people could only travel with this assurance of safety, that they wouldn't be murdered in their beds for extending or accepting hospitality.

In classical times, all strangers had the right to hospitality. Without even sharing their names, they were offered food, clothing, and gifts. Greek myth relies on this sacred law, and those who broke hospitality to attack a guest or host were cursed (this concept appears in the Iliad and Odyssey both). Zeus was called Zeus Xenios, guarantor of hospitality and protector of guests.

This tradition may seem extreme or outmoded to modern readers, but in ancient times it was incontrovertible for moral people. In the Bible, Lot is prepared to sacrifice his daughters to an angry mob rather than give them his guests, and Abraham made a point of running down the road to beg every traveler to stop in for a meal. Middle Eastern tradition is clear on this issue, and even the captain of the forty thieves in Arabian Nights refuses to eat salt rather than accept this guest-right and then murder his host.

Europe of course has strong roots in the classical

tradition. Dante's Divine Comedy names those who break guest-right the second worst kind of traitors, condemned to the lowest level of hell. *The Hobbit* references this trope – even irritating dwarves who show up from nowhere must be feasted. The Count of Monte Cristo refuses to eat in his enemy's house. Macbeth worries about killing his king, a guest in his castle, and certainly everything he does subsequently is cursed. Ivanhoe and King Arthur, especially *Gawain and the Green Knight*, use this concept. Basically, in classical, Biblical, and the medieval tradition founded on them, this really meant something. Parts of this tradition, like taking a fight outside the building where one is eating or staying, still remain. (Frankel, *Winning the Game* 48)

When Mance Rayder meets Jon, he notes, "The laws of hospitality are as old as the First Men, and sacred as a heart tree" (III.102). It remains to be seen whether an ancient curse will take down the Freys.

Chestnuts

Cersei serves chestnut soup to Tyrion while holding his lover (as she thinks) hostage. "Chestnuts seem to be a foil to the queen: while the raw, spiny fruit looks ominous to the passerby, Cersei's menace is less apparent, except to those who know her as well as Tyrion does" (Kistler 98). There's a chestnut seller crying his wares during her walk of shame. Likewise, Lord Manderly serves venison with chestnuts to the Freys. In both scenes, elegance and concealed malice are key – the attack comes, not from the food, but from another quarter. Chestnuts are also a fall food, like the frequent apples, as well as corn, pumpkin soup, grapes, and squash served in the series.

Dates and Figs

Dates and figs are sweet but also dry. Thus they're a symbol of endurance in the desert but also withering. Daenerys calls for dates when she awakens from her book one miscarriage, before she learns she's lost the baby.

The fig, associated with Eden, symbolizes fertility, loss of innocence, and a fall from grace. Daenerys eats figs and dates in Meereen, as the city seethes under her rule. Lady Olenna also eats figs, sharing them with those who plot treachery against her. While plotting in the game of thrones, Arianne Martell serves a snack in the desert of dates, cheese and olives. Dates conceal pits, and figs, seeds, so Kistler calls dates "a perfect treat for those who present one face on the outside and prove to have different intentions" (60).

Grapes

Across the noisy common room, Salladhor Saan sat eating grapes from a wooden bowl. When he spied Davos, he beckoned him closer.

"Ser knight, come sit with me. Eat a grape. Eat two. They are marvelously sweet." [...] "Are you sure that you will not have a grape? Children go hungry in the city, it is said." He dangled the grapes before Davos and smiled.

"It's ale I need, and news."

> "The men of Westeros are ever rushing," complained Salladhor Saan. "What good is this, I ask you? He who hurries through life hurries to his grave." He belched. "The Lord of Casterly Rock has sent his dwarf to see to King's Landing. Perhaps he hopes that his ugly face will frighten off attackers, eh? Or that we will laugh ourselves dead when the Imp capers on the battlements, who can say? The dwarf has chased off the lout who ruled the gold cloaks and put in his place a knight with an iron hand." He plucked a grape, and squeezed it between thumb and forefinger until the skin burst. Juice ran down between his fingers. (II.152-153) .

Salladhor Saan describes how eager he is for war, as red juice runs down his fingers before the Battle of Blackwater. The symbolism is clear. Grapes represent fertility and sacrifice, the latter from their bloody color (Cirlot 121). Later Littlefinger offers Sansa an assortment of fruit, including "sad-looking grapes" (III.933). She is sick of war, blood, and all that accompanies it.

Lambs and Sheep

In the Judeo-Christian traditions, a lamb was a possession of high value, thus an appropriate sacrifice to God. The Lhazareen, or Lamb Men, are famously slaughtered in the first book, leaving Daenerys to try to save them. "The Dothraki horselords call the Lhazareen the Lamb Men. When you shear them all they do is bleat. They are not a martial people," Xaro says (V.210).

Ser Barristan's Lhazareen squire, the Red Lamb, announces in a released chapter of *The Winds of Winter* that if he dies he will stand before his god, the Great Shepherd of Lhazar, break his crook, and ask, "Why did you make your people lambs when the world is full of wolves?" House Stokeworth, with its sigil of a lamb and motto of "Proud to be Faithful" fares just as badly in the war. Their half-witted daughter Lollys is raped repeatedly then married to a vicious sellsword. Cersei uses them as catspaws, resulting in more and more deaths.

The Hound appalls Arya by accepting a farmer's meal of lamb stew, then stealing all his treasure. He defends his act by saying the family will clearly be dead by winter. As the Hound adds in the books, "If there are gods, they made sheep so wolves could eat mutton, and they made the weak for the strong to play with" (II.757). Daenerys's dragons prey on the countryfolk's sheep, emphasizing this fact and making her choose what kind of ruler she wishes to become. Likewise, Ygritte's sheepskins look more cuddly than tough, though she can certainly defend herself. Sam dreams of "a leg of lamb. A whole leg, just for me" before his friends leave him for the White Walkers (II.367).

Lamb is the last and best-cooked dish served at the red wedding, just before everyone's slaughtered. In the House of the Undying, Dany dreams of Robb: "On a throne above them sat a dead man with the head of a wolf. He wore an iron crown and held a leg of lamb in one hand as a king might hold a sceptre, and his eyes followed Dany with mute appeal" (II.700).

Jon and his friends eat lamb before they take their oath as Black Brothers, emphasizing their youth as they're sacrificed for the realm. Tyrion actually requests lamb while trapped in Lysa Arryn's sky cell. Illyrio serves Tyrion lamb and Tyrion worries that

Illyrio will sacrifice him to the Lannisters. Melisandre treats Gendry as her sacrificial lamb:

> Melisandre: Have you ever slaughtered a lamb, my king?
> Stannis: No.
> Melisandre: If the lamb sees the knife, she panics. Her panic seeps into her meat, darkens it, fouls the flavor.
> Stannis: You've slaughtered many lambs?
> Melisandre: And none have seen the blade ("Second Sons")

Daenerys later punishes Ser Jorah, and then dines on lamb (III.992). On another occasion, she says, "I may be a young girl innocent of war, but I am not a lamb to walk bleating into the harpy's den" (V.403). Nonetheless she does, joining the Green Grace for supper and even eating lamb with her.

Lamprey

Lord Manderly, sometimes called Lord Lamprey, consumes enormous amounts of lamprey pie in decadent self-indulgence, emphasizing his wealth and coastal holdings. The lamprey was a popular dinner fish from the Middle Ages, and also a parasite. Henry I of England was said to have died from gorging himself on steamed lampreys. Manderly, who rules White Harbor beside the sea, serves lamprey several times, suggesting his wealth and choice of home as well as his parasitic nature. Lady Tanda Stokeworth serves lamprey, with similar associations, as she tries to wheedle lords into marrying her unappealing daughter. "Manderly feeds Davos lamprey to send him a message about his real intent, and to soften him up for an arduous mission to Cannibal Island. Lady Tanda offers lamprey pie to entice a husband for Lollys; a hard sell, that one. Lamprey does seem to indicate luxury" ("The Food Code of Ice and Fire").

It's used to butter people up in the books. Davos, imprisoned, is thrilled to be offered a too-rich lamprey pie while imprisoned by Stannis, because it suggests he still has friends. Ser Balon Swann refuses the lamprey pie that he's served in Dorne – he's not prepared to be bought off or pacified. It's said of the fat, corrupt High Septon of the second book, "He bathes in scented waters and grows fat on lark and lamprey while his people starve!" (II.317). Littlefinger loves the dish and seeks it out at taverns. "But serving the likes of Littlefinger a dish of eel as slippery as he may not produce the intended consequences..." (Kistler 152).

Lemons

Lemons seem to signify innocence or the old ways of living, now passed beyond forever. In medieval times, lemons were prized summery fruits, difficult to obtain in the cold regions of Europe.

Naive Sansa loves lemoncakes, but she's also the most attached to the old tales – she dreams of wedding a handsome prince from the ballads. The Tyrells make a point of serving her lemoncakes when they ask her to wed their heir and become a lady of Highgarden. She immediately begins spinning fantasies of a life of love and pleasure among gardens, puppies, and children. "The lemon is a symbol of fidelity in love, and, as such, is associated with the Virgin Mary" (Ferguson 33). As a sign of propriety and the virgin, the association ties in well with religious symbolism, as does the cheery yellow color. Sansa begins the story cheerful, naive and loyal, even choosing Joffrey's side over Arya's in "The Kingsroad."

Arya in turn wants a lemon bun when she's alone in King's Landing and missing her sister. She must bathe in lemonwater to scrub off the fish scent from being Cat of the Canals, but part of her must also long for a simpler, fresher time.

Dany has a recurring memory of the lemon tree beside her childhood house with the red door. Robin Arryn loves lemoncakes, particularly when he's told he must leave his home. Lem Lemoncloak reminisces about a duck cooked with lemons from his youth, though he doesn't get it. He and his band (led by Beric Dondarrion) are knights of the old code, dedicated to protecting the helpless in a world without chivalry.

The Old Bear always drinks his beer with lemon juice:

> Jon opened a shuttered window, took the flagon of beer off the outside ledge, and filled a horn. Hobb had given him a lemon, still cold from the Wall. Jon crushed in his fist. The juice trickled through his fingers. Mormont drank lemon in his beer every day, and claimed that it was why he still had his own teeth. (I.781)

In this scene, Mormont discusses Jon's desertion with him – just after Jon has tried returning to his childhood family. Mormont too represents the old ways, a way that will soon pass on forever.

After Cersei hears good news about the war, she kisses Tyrion on the cheek. "Tyrion Lannister could not have been more astonished if Aegon the Conqueror himself had burst into the room, riding on a dragon and juggling lemon pies" (II.320). While this comment is meant to emphasize the ridiculous factor, Tyrion is also being nostalgic about family, surrounded as he is by contempt. When Lord Mormont tells Sam he doesn't care if the old Maesters called dragonglass lemon pie – he wants it, he's also looking to the past. Of course, nostalgia can be misleading:

> Robert: Those were the days!
> Renly: Which days, exactly? The ones when half of Westeros fought the other half and millions died? Or before that, when the Mad King slaughtered women and babies because the voices in his head told him they deserved it? Or way before that, when dragons burnt whole cities to the ground?
> Robert: Easy boy, you might be my brother, but you're speaking to the king.
> Renly: I suppose it was all rather heroic, if you were drunk enough and had some poor Riverlands whore to shove your prick inside and "make the eight." ("A Golden Crown")

Aside from the nostalgia connection, lemons have a strong, sour taste. It's unsurprising that Stannis likes lemon water, as his entire personality is sour. The chilling Darkstar of Dorne also drinks "unsweetened lemonwater" (IV.300). Upon hearing of a tragic death, Cersei drinks water with "lemon squeezings so tart she spit it out" (IV.47). Thus they can be a symbol of bitterness and resentment, as well of one of longing for the past.

Nuts

Rickon endlessly smashes nuts on the table as Bran holds court in "The Ghost of Harrenhal." As he pounds, he shows his violence and fury at being abandoned by his family, one by one. While other characters eat nuts on occasion, especially chestnuts, there are few significant nut scenes. Nuts, like seeds, represent potential for growth – Rickon is a nut himself, which could grow into a mighty tree if allowed the chance.

Olives

> The olive figures prominently in the myths and customs of Greece, in particular, where it served as a symbol of peace and of constancy; an emblem of achievement; and a sacred, immortal, and divine fruit... Because the olive had to suffer (to be pressed) in order to produce riches (oil), the Greeks made it a symbol of victory over adversity. They also made it a symbol of regeneration and included it in immortality myths. Olive trees appeared to be immortal. They were known to live for centuries. (Andrews 163)

An olive branch famously represents peace in western culture, alluding back to the story of Noah's Ark. When Daenerys advances on Meereen, the nobles burn the olive trees in a scorched-earth tactic. After the battle, with no slaves and no olives (their biggest export), the Meereenese economy is in ruins, as so often happens in war. Daenerys plants many olive trees, hoping for strength in adversity, but the trees are slow to grow.

When Xaro visits Dany he tells her that he will take all of the olives and olive oil she's willing to sell. She replies that they're replanting the trees but it will take decades before the olive industry is restored. In just this way, true lasting peace has been disrupted and it will take much time to rebuild. Likewise, the peace she enjoyed with Qarth is shattered. A mercenary leader tells Griff and his friends that Daenerys "seems more intent on planting olive trees than in reclaiming her father's throne" of Westeros (V.315). Literally and symbolically, this is in fact true.

When Dany eats breakfast on the day she marries, she's nibbling on an olive that Missandei has brought her while she makes the final choice to bring peace to her people. On her throne, Daenerys often eats olives with cheese and flatbread – simple foods with a simple hope for peace that is so often denied to her. Thinking she can stage a bloodless coup, Arianne Martell serves her friends olives in Dorne.

In the wilderness, Daenerys thinks that dragons don't plant olive trees, nor do Dothraki – it takes leaving Meereen and its fledgling orchards to remember that she is not truly a peace-bringer, but a dragon, who brings fire and blood.

Onions

Onions, whenever they're mentioned, blend the good of humanity with the bad of humanity, emphasizing how people all have shares of both. This likely nods to an onion's many layers.

Of course, Davos, the humble Onion Knight, takes his standard from the food he brought to Stannis. Famously, Stannis rewarded the hero side of him and punished the smuggler, acknowledging Davos's good side beside the bad. Melisandre uses the roots to demonstrate her fanatical philosophy concerning men: if a part of the onion is rotten, then the whole onion is rotten. Of course, she appears incorrect about human nature.

The onion was a humble, working-class food in Europe, much like the Onion Knight himself. Thus humble Benjen Stark eats one at Winterfell as Jon proposes joining the Watch (I.52). Jon will soon have many awakenings about mankind's real nature, good and bad.

> The offensive odor of the onion led many to fear its power. Its appearance and structure, however, fostered a different view: The onion was likened by some to a pearl-gold on the outside and white on the inside; and like a pearl, they thought, it symbolized oneness and unity. Furthermore, the onion was spherical in shape, consisting of a series of orbs, one inside the other.
> (Andrews 164-165)

Aside from their strong scent (believed to be proof against demons), onions are best known for their layer effect, discussed between the Onion Knight, Stannis and Melisandre. People are not all good or all evil, but as Martin always shows, they're complex with many pieces to them, each layer below another. It's possible Davos will succeed in teaching his leaders this lesson.

Brienne drinks onion broth with the Brotherhood Without Banners, who have fallen on disturbing times in the fourth book. Nonetheless, some of them still have kindness and honor. Arya watches a moneylender drink onion broth, as the Kindly Man tells her the moneylender "is a man like any other, with light in him and darkness" (V.838).

Jon smells the onion on Ygritte's breath when he first meets her and must decide whether to kill this woman who's only technically his enemy as he finds himself liking her. She is his first of many lessons that the Wildlings are no different than he is, with the same gods and values. Jon eats onions for lunch and dinner before the Wildlings attack the wall and he must kill his comrades. Onion soup is served when the free folk join the alliance, again emphasizing that they're just people, not necessarily all heroes or all villains. Finally, Jon tells them they have a choice who they will become: soldiers for the Black Brothers or starving free folk:

> The black brothers began to pass out food. They'd brought slabs of hard salt beef, dried cod, dried beans, turnips, carrots, sacks of barley meal and wheaten flour, pickled eggs, barrels of onions and apples. "You can have an onion or an apple," Jon heard Hairy Hal tell one woman, "but not both. You got to pick." [...]
> "Hal, what was it that you told this woman?"
> Hal looked confused. "About the food, you mean? An apple or an onion? that's all I said. They got to pick."
> "You have to pick," Jon Snow repeated. "All of you.[...]those who want to help us hold the Wall, return to Castle Black with me and I'll see you armed and fed. The rest of you, get your turnips and your onions and crawl back inside your holes." (V.273-274)

Peaches

> Q. In the second book Renly gives Stannis a peach. What did you want to tell us with that?
> GRRM: The peach represents... Well... It's pleasure. It's...tasting the juices of life. Stannis is a very marshal men concerned with his duty and with that peach Renly says: "Smell the roses," because Stannis is always concerned with his duty and honor, in what he should be doing and he never really stops to taste the fruit. Renly wants him to taste the fruit but it's lost. I wish that scene had been included in the TV series because for me that peach was important, but it wasn't possible. ("A Very Long Interview")

In fact, driven by guilt and confusion, Stannis focuses on that peach for a long time after. He tells Davos:

> Renly offered me a peach. At our parley. Mocked me, defied me, threatened me, and offered me a peach. I thought he was drawing a blade and went for mine own. Was that his purpose, to make me show fear? Or was it one of his pointless jests? When he spoke of how sweet the peach was, did his words have some hidden meaning?" The king gave a shake of his head, like a dog shaking a rabbit to snap its neck. "Only Renly could vex me so with a piece of fruit. He brought his doom on himself with his treason, but I did love him, Davos. I know that now. I swear, I will go to my grave thinking of my brother's peach. (II.613-614)

Stannis is so far removed from youth, frivolity, and desire that he cannot even comprehend Renly's offer.

Robert and Pycelle both mention peaches as belonging to the "good old days," a time of past adventures in the south and warm summers.

> "You need to come south," Robert told [Ned]. "You need a taste of summer before it flees. In Highgarden there are fields of golden roses that stretch away as far as the eye can see. The fruits are so ripe they explode in your mouth – melons, peaches, fireplums, you've never tasted such sweetness. (I.41)

The peach suggests a summery pleasure, one that will not last long because winter is coming. In fact, Robert will die before the season changes. This echoes Renly's identity as one of the "knights of summer," unaware of the pain of war. Many young men's beards are called "peach fuzz," emphasizing the same imagery. Similarly, Bran compares climbing to the sweetness of a peach – something he soon loses forever. "He liked the deep, sweet ache it left in the muscles afterward. He liked the way the air tasted way up high, sweet and cold as a winter peach. He liked the birds" (I.81).

When Joffrey puts her aside, Sansa naively thinks that her troubles are over and remarks about how sweet the food, including peaches, tastes. Of course, she doesn't realize that she's still a Lannister pawn. Arya arrives at the Peach Inn with the Brotherhood, thinking she's safe before Sandor Clegane appears. Dany's arc frequently mentions peaches – Ser Jorah brings her a peach in Vaes Tolloro, the City of Ghosts, and she remarks on how sweet it tastes in a temporary respite from the Red Waste. Soon enough, they leave for Qarth.

> "I've brought you a peach," Ser Jorah said, kneeling. It was so small she could almost hide it in her palm, and overripe too, but when she took the first bite, the flesh was so sweet she almost cried. She ate it slowly, savoring every mouthful, while Ser Jorah told her of the tree it had been plucked from, in a garden near the western wall.
>
> "Fruit and water and shade," Dany said, her cheeks sticky with peach juice. "The gods were good to bring us to this place." (II.196) .

The slavemaster in Astapor smells like peaches, but Dany realizes she can outsmart him – the downfall of Astapor is close at hand. Tyrion notices peaches are served at Joffrey's wedding, just before tragedy strikes. Likewise, Asha remembers eating peaches with her beloved years before:

90

When she made him try a bite, the juice ran down his chin, and she had to kiss it clean. That night they'd spent devouring peaches and each other, and by the time daylight returned Asha was sated and sticky and as happy as she'd ever been. Was that six years ago, or seven? Summer was a fading memory, and it had been three years since Asha last enjoyed a peach. (V.335)

Pears

"Pomegranate seeds were so messy; Sansa chose a pear instead, and took a small delicate bite. It was very ripe. The juice ran down her chin." Pear trees can be a symbol of love but also independence because they're sweet and self-pollinating. Viserion lazily curls around a pear tree and knocks a fruit at Daenerys in the fifth book, possibly cautioning her to remain bloodless and celibate. "Some Europeans also recognize longevity and even immortality in their pears. A Gaelic legend referred to apples of Avalon as pears, and these fruits grew in paradise and held the secret to everlasting life" (Andrews 172).

"People in much of Europe viewed the pear as a symbol of fertility and womanhood. The fruit had a shape similar to that of a woman's body as well as that of the womb" (Andrews 172). There was a custom in Europe to plant a pear tree for each girl and an apple tree for each boy. In many cultures, the pear represents the human heart because of its shape. Dany commands Daario to eat a pear when he hasn't eaten for two days and declares feasting on her beauty is enough to sustain him (V.302). While she offers it to him out of affection, she must be cautious and true to herself rather than giving away her heart to one unworthy.

Spicy Peppers

"In the Queen's Ballroom they broke their fast on honeycakes baked with blackberries and nuts, gammon steaks, bacon, fingerfish crisped in breadcrumbs, autumn pears, and a Dornish dish of onions, cheese, and chopped eggs cooked up with fiery peppers" (III.802). This is before Joffrey's wedding, suggesting the chaos and turmoil to come. "Crabs boiled in fiery eastern spices" are served at the wedding in a parade of seventy-seven opulent courses (III.820).

Spicy peppers are emblematic of Dorne and its cuisine of course but also of the fiery chaos of war and the angry feelings stirring at many supper tables. Tyrion eats fiery peppers and applecakes before his trial in book three (965). Ser Barristan recalls the dragon peppers he ate the day he was knighted. "His passion for serving his king – or queen – is no less strong than it was the day he first knelt before Aegon the Unlikely" (Kistler 175). The spiciest stew of all, with seven kinds of vipers and venom, appears when the Dornish receive a delivery of an enemy's head.

Persimmons

Daenerys has a persimmon tree at her palace in Meereen in the books. Quaithe comes to her beneath the tree to warn her enemies are coming. In a similar scene, Missandei suggests Dany not go to the fighting pits as the persimmon tree is shadowing the rising sun. Whenever persimmons appear, Daenerys must compromise her ethics and position further. The orange color of sovereignty and sticky sweetness of the fruit bear a high price, it seems. In Astapor, Daenerys negotiates with the slavers over persimmon wine.

> I must have them all. Dany knew what she must do now, though the taste of it was so bitter that even the persimmon wine could not cleanse it from her mouth. She had considered long and hard and found no other way. It is my only choice. "Give me all," she said, "and you may have a dragon." (III.370)

"She was breaking her fast on a bowl of cold shrimp-and-persimmon soup when Irri brought her a Qartheen gown, an airy confection of ivory samite patterned with seed pearls" [sky blue on the show] (II.870). Daenerys decides in this scene to leave Qarth with no ship and no army.

Later Xaro returns and meets with her. "Xaro perused the fruits on the platter Jhiqui offered him and chose a persimmon. Its orange skin matched the color of the coral in his nose. He took a bite and pursed his lips. 'Tart'" (V.204). He reminds her she is losing her hold over the people in Meereen and rejects her offers.

Pie
At Dany's wedding to Drogo, there are Dothraki blood pies. Beautiful doves burst from the wedding pie in the show, but Joffrey hacks at least one dead with his sword, as he so often does to peace itself. In the books, Tyrion complains that the entire reception will be a rain of bird droppings. Peace is ugly and defiled in

King's Landing. Upon savagely slicing open his wedding pie, Joffrey chokes on it. He can bring no more damage to the peace process.

After bidding goodbye to his Frey guests, Manderly serves three particularly disturbing meat pies at a wedding and calls for a song about the Rat King. Significantly, the Rat King was known for baking his enemy's son in a pie and serving it to him. As Bran tells it:

> When the king was visiting the Nightfort, the cook killed the king's son, cooked him into a big pie with onions, carrots, mushrooms and bacon. That night he served the pie to the king. He liked the taste of his son so much, he asked for a second slice. The gods turned the cook into a giant white rat who could only eat his own young. He's been roaming the Nightfort ever since, devouring his own babies. But no matter what he does, he's always hungry. ("Mhysa")

Pie, known for hiding its contents, suggests an unpleasant surprise rather than a pleasant one. Littlefinger comments of his schemes, "If the pie is opened, the birds begin to sing, and Varys wouldn't like that" (I.200). Stew, also called a "bowl o' brown" in the pot shops of Flea Bottom, has just as disturbing a reputation, especially after Tyrion has someone made into "singer's stew."

Pigeon

Pigeons are eaten several times in the story, most obviously when Arya is alone in King's Landing just before her father's death. While on the show she appears a bit hapless (no one wants to buy her raw, dead pigeon), in the book she gets by, trading half of each pigeon to a pot shop in return for giving her dinner and toasting the other half in their oven. Pigeons wander urban areas, bobbing heedlessly and picking up whatever they can. Thus they represent the lost culture of the young generation, as well as ignorance and gossip. Arya, alone on the streets, must beware all of this and find the courage to discover a path for herself. Joffrey chokes on pigeon pie in his wedding of the books, suggesting that he too has allowed the city to corrupt his thinking and elevate him past the thought of consequences.

Pike

The pike, a sharp-toothed carnivorous fish, is served several times in the series.

In the market, Tyrion comes across fishwives selling pikes at inflated prices:

> The fishwives did more business than all the rest combined. Buyers flocked around the barrels and stalls to haggle over winkles, clams, and river pike. With no other food coming into the city, the price of fish was ten times what it had been before the war, and still rising. (II.534)

Deception, greed, and plotting surround the vicious creature.

> In what can hardly be a coincidence, a herb-crusted pike is served only twice in the entire story and in two identical situations. Amerei Frey offers it to Jaime when she is asking him to kill Beric for her and Cersei is feeding it (among other dishes) to Ser Balman when she is asking him to get rid of [someone] for her. ("The Food Code of Ice and Fire")

> The serving men were bringing out the fish course, a river pike baked in a crust of herbs and crushed nuts.

Lancel's lady tasted it, approved, and commanded that the first portion be served to Jaime. As they set the fish before him, she leaned across her husband's place to touch his golden hand. "You could kill Lord Beric, Ser Jaime. You slew the Smiley Knight. Please, my lord, I beg you, stay and help us with Lord Beric and the Hound." (IV.452)

"I beg you, ser," [Cersei] whispered, "do not make me say it..."
"I understand." Ser Balman raised a finger.
"You are a true knight indeed, ser. The answer to a frightened mother's prayers." The rest was hippocras and buttered beets, hot-baked bread, herb-crusted pike, and ribs of wild boar. (IV.360)

The carnivorous fish is hidden under its herb crust, suggesting the deception and hypocrisy of the violence the highborn lady is suggesting. The hippocras (hot spiced red wine) and red beets suggest blood, while wild boar nods to the previous treachery Cersei committed by murdering King Robert.

At the wedding feast of the Dunk and Egg short story "The Mystery Knight" there's a pike crusted with crushed almonds (674). In fact, everyone there is plotting treason. Pike is likewise hidden in almond milk and served at the Red Wedding. All the Freys are deceiving the Starks there, with the crying Roslyn presented as bait.

After Cersei's walk of shame, she dines with Ser Kevan on plain roasted pike. She has lost her "outer coverings" and some of her appearance at innocence, but she clearly plans to continue her plots. At the same meal, Tommen serves "morsels of pike off his own royal plate" to his kittens while gossiping about the "bad cat" that's stalking them (V.955). If pike suggests betrayal and deception through self-interest, Tommen's enemies are closing in.

Daenerys is offered pike in Meereen. "A pike of unprecedented size had been caught in the Skahazadhan, and the fisherman wished to give it to the queen. She admired the fish extravagantly, rewarded the fisherman with a purse of silver, and sent the pike to her kitchens" (V.43). While this moment seems benign, the people of her city still seethe under her rule. A few gifts are no substitute for loyalty.

By contrast, Alys Karstark refuses pike at her wedding and goes to dance with her new husband. She means to be a true wife without an agenda or the need for deception.

Plums and Prunes

Plums are symbols of duplicity and betrayal, appearing several times in the series.

Illyrio, Varys' partner in plotting, eats suckling pig in plum sauce. Lord Bolton eats prunes and presses them on Ser Jaime several times. Dolorous Ed warns Jon, "Never trust a cook, my lord. They'll prune you when you least expect it" (V.47). At the banquet where Viserys is crowned with molten gold, "Half-clothed women spun and danced on the low tables, amid joints of meat and platters piled high with plums and dates and pomegranates" (I.494). Cersei fills Sansa's glass with plum wine during the Battle of Blackwater and divulges her plan for Ser Ilyn to kill them all. At the purple wedding of season four, plums surround a suckling pig on a table, and as it's reported in the books, the corpse's face was "black as a plum" (III.843).

Of course, Brown Ben Plumm defects more than once, thus living up to his own name. Maynard Plumm in the short story "The Mystery Knight" is an ambiguous figure who only calls himself "a friend" but appears to spy for the King's Hand (718).

After Jon's midnight ride to desert the Black Brothers and join Robb, he brings the Old Bear breakfast: "Today it was three brown eggs boiled hard, with fried bread and ham steak and a bowl of wrinkled plums" (I.781). They discuss his betrayal and commitment to the Watch. Finally, Theon's father plots his own betrayal:

> Lord Balon laughed. "Well, at the least you are no craven. No more than I'm a fool. Do you think I gather my ships to watch them rock at anchor? I mean to carve out a kingdom with fire and sword... but not from the west, and not at the bidding of King Robb the Boy. Casterly Rock is too strong, and Lord Tywin too cunning by half. Aye, we might take Lannisport, but we should never keep it. No. I hunger for a different plum... not so juicy sweet, to be sure, yet it hangs there ripe and undefended."
> Where? Theon might have asked, but by then he knew. (II.186)

Under his father's direction, Theon attacks his friends at Winterfell.

Pomegranates

A pomegranate with its many seeds can symbolize pregnancy and fertility as well as its deadly bloody color. In early Christian art, the Virgin Mary is often depicted with a pomegranate, symbolizing her power over death and new life. They symbolize eternal life and divine prosperity, but also sin and a fall from grace.

> Myths and legends of the pomegranate reveal that the ancients both recognized and revered this fruit. The plant comes from Southeast Asia, and the fruit itself appears in myths of many lands, particularly of India, China, Mesopotamia, Greece, and Rome. The pomegranate had distinct characteristics that beckoned mythmakers to assign it significance. It attracted attention because of its crownlike blossom, its red color, and perhaps most importantly, its many seeds, which people all over the world linked to fertility and procreation. Ancient mythmakers elevated pomegranates to high status, attributing symbolic significance to all of these traits. (Andrews 181)

While the seeds reminded the ancients of fertility, its bloody color and juice were just as significant. At the banquet where Viserys is crowned with molten gold, "Half-clothed women spun and danced on the low tables, amid joints of meat and platters piled high with plums and dates and pomegranates" (I.494). Xaro serves Dany wine that tastes of them, gifts her with them, and betrays her. At the fighting pits of Meereen, "Hizdahr had stocked their box with flagons of chilled wine and sweetwater, with figs, dates, melons, and pomegranates, with pecans and peppers and a big bowl of honeyed locusts," refreshments to enjoy while men die (V.691). Sickened by the bloodshed, Dany eats only the figs and dates.

Bowen Marsh, steward of the Wall, is called the "Old Pomegranate" for his coloring. As it turns out, he can be deadly as well. Dolorous Ed describes him saying, "Pomegranates. All those seeds. A man could choke to death. I'd sooner have a turnip. Never knew a turnip to do a man any harm" (V.268). A turnip of course is bloodless.

Michele Clapton created Sansa's wedding dress with an embroidered band that symbolically told Sansa's life from her Tully and Stark origins to the entanglement with the Lannisters. Red pomegranates emphasize the growing Lannister influence over her. Meanwhile, the blood-soaked Lannisters are wrapping themselves around her until she's wed in their colors, though with a touch of wolves still present.

After whisking her away, Littlefinger offers Sansa half a pomegranate, which Sansa worriedly declines. "Pomegranate seeds were so messy; Sansa chose a pear instead, and took a small delicate bite" (III.933). Most fans read this as his offering her a share in his bloodshed or other Faustian bargain. In Greek myth, Hades the god of death offered innocent Persephone a pomegranate of blood and fertility – by accepting, she was trapped in the underworld as death's bride.

Red Wine

Melisandre offers Gendry good wine in "Second Sons," then attacks him and brutally takes his blood for her sacrifice magic. While red wine appears so often in the series – book and show – that all the instances cannot be listed, wine certainly has the appearance of blood. At particular times, it symbolizes it as well.

The wine seller in the Dothraki market tries to poison Daenerys with Dornish red. Lord Kevan, Cersei's uncle, rejects her request for aid at a meal where "A last drop of wine trembled wet and red beneath his chin, and finally fell" (IV.115). Bolton tries not to get his hands bloody, despite his treachery:

> Jaime: Shall we drink on it?
> Bolton: I don't partake.
> Jaime: You do understand how suspicious that is to ordinary people? ("The Climb")

Though he is peripheral to the Red Wedding, he betrays his king, Robb Stark, supports the Lannisters, and marries a granddaughter of treacherous Lord Frey.

SYMBOLS IN GAME OF THRONES

SEASONS SKY AND WEATHER

Autumn

During Daenerys's final chapter in the fifth book, she notes that the Dothraki Sea is drying up in the onrushing autumn. Thus autumn can indicate a transience, an ending. The symbolism of leaves falling and animals preparing to hibernate often stands for deterioration, death, and dying. It can also symbolize the maturity and understanding the young characters are achieving. By this point, they're no longer children.

"Tragedy is the *mythos* of autumn" (Westfahl 57) – the world is dying and hope dies along with it. Thus Ned's and Drogo's deaths herald the change of seasons, as the Stark children scatter and Daenerys faces the fire. When the white raven brings news of autumn, Stannis marshals his forces, kills his brother the heedless "knight of summer," and suffers defeat at Blackwater Bay. Martin's episode "The Bear and the Maiden Fair" was originally called "Autumn Storms" as the characters head toward conflict. The terrible weddings of the third book and all take place in autumn, as does Daenerys's violent campaign in Slaver's Bay.

"Winter storms are worse but autumn's are more frequent," Cotter Pyke says (IV.217). This may prove prophetic about the war, as the many battles must slow when deep snow falls, but the Long Night of the Others will fall.

Comet

> Everyone associates the red comet of *A Clash of Kings* with their own rise to power: King Joffrey sees Lannister red; Edmure Tully, Tully red. Brynden Tully, Aeron Greyjoy, and Osha all see an omen of war and bloodshed. Old Nan, whose ancient stories prove true, senses the coming of dragons. Certainly, the comet appears when Daenerys enters the fire and brings her dragons to life. But as it begins the second book, it also warns readers of the arrival of R'hllor, the god of fire, and his Red Priestess Melisandre. With her, magic arrives at Westeros. Her prophecies as she leads troops in the name of fire, against the mysterious Other, may be the best magic to battle the ice. (Frankel, *Winter is Coming*)

In King's Landing it's called "King Joffrey's Comet" at court and "Dragon's Tail" in the streets. Among the Night's Watch, it is known as "Mormont's Torch." The Greyjoys and Tullys as well as the Greatjon see it as a summons to war, and each proclaims it's on their side. "The sighting of a comet was always supposed to herald dire events on earth" (Walker 338).

> Brynden Tully, Aeron Greyjoy, and Osha all see it as a portent of war and bloodshed; and to near-blind Old Nan, who claims she can smell it, the red comet means the coming of dragons. In a sense, what the fire portends to the reader is R'hllor, the Lord of Light, and his priestess, Melisandre. (Scoble 134)

Since it first appears for readers when Daenerys steps into the bonfire, readers tend to believe it portends the dragons and a return of magic to the world. However, as often happens, readers may not have the whole picture. Certainly, the dragons and comet coincide with the dawn of war, and it may be the dragons that end it (or as Martin has joked, the comet may flatten them all).

Among the Faith it is known as the "Sword that Slays the Season": autumn is coming and a time of war as well. Theon tells his uncle Aeron that the Faith calls it "A herald of a new age. A messenger from the gods," but Aeron replies that the drowned Gods have sent it:

> A burning brand it is, such as our people carried of old. It is the flame the Drowned God brought from the sea, and it proclaims a rising tide. It is time to hoist our sails and go forth into the world with fire and sword, as he did. (II.179)

Daenerys knows it arrived with her dragons and follows it through the Red Waste. Many of her people die there, but it leads her to Qarth and the visions of Quaithe. In one vision in the House of the Undying, the Undying Ones claim to have sent the comet to guide her to them (II.704).

When asked about the comet at the Battle of Hastings, Martin replies, "The comet was actually more drawn from the Bard's in *Julius Caesar*, as well as the ones actually in the sky as I was writing" ("So Spake Martin" C91, P45). Act 2, scene 2 of *Julius Caesar* proclaims, "When beggars die there are no comets seen./ The heavens themselves blaze forth the death of princes" (30-31). In history, one of the brightest comets ever seen blazed across the sky after Caesar's death, proclaiming to his people that he had become a god. Daenerys's comet is not for a death but a birth as she becomes the Mother of Dragons and more than merely mortal.

In the tales of King Arthur, Uther Pendragon took his name from a comet, this one tied to dragons. When he saw it in the sky, he knew his royal destiny: His children would rule the known world. Daenerys may have the same fate.

> There appeared a star of wonderful magnitude and brightness, darting forth a ray, at the end of which was a globe of fire in form of a dragon, out of whose mouth issued forth two rays; one of which seemed to stretch out itself beyond the extent of Gaul, the other towards the Irish Sea, and ended in seven lesser rays. ... At the appearance of this star, a general fear and amazement seized the people; and even Uther, the king's brother, who was then upon his march with his army into Cambria, being not a little terrified at it, was very curious to know of the learned men, what it portended. Among others, he ordered Merlin to be called, who also attended in this expedition to give his advice in the management of the war; and who, now being presented before him, was commanded to discover to him the significance of the star. At this he burst out into tears, and with a loud voice cried out, "O irreparable loss! O distressed people of

Britain! Alas! the illustrious prince is departed! The renowned king of the Britons, Aurelius Ambrosius, is dead! whose death will prove fatal to us all, unless God be our helper. Make haste, therefore, most noble Uther, make haste to engage the enemy: the victory will be yours, and you shall be king of all Britain. For the star, and the fiery dragon under it, signifies yourself, and the ray extending towards the Gallic coast, portends that you shall have a most potent son, to whose power all those kingdoms shall be subject over which the ray reaches. But the other ray signifies a daughter, whose sons and grandsons shall successively enjoy the kingdom of Britain." (Geoffrey of Monmouth)

Dawn/Morning

"Make no mistake, good sers and valiant brothers, the war we've come to fight is no petty squabble over lands and honors. Ours is a war for life itself, and should we fail the world dies with us."
...
All of them seemed surprised to hear Maester Aemon murmur, "It is the war for the dawn you speak of, my lady. But where is the prince that was promised?"
"He stands before you," Melisandre declared, "though you do not have the eyes to see it. Stannis Baratheon is Azor Ahai come again, the warrior of fire." (III.884)

Thus the upcoming battle of ice and fire, against the unending night is called (unsurprisingly) the War for the Dawn in Melisandre's lore. It's called this elsewhere, as in a song sung at the Winterfell harvest feast "the Night's Watch rode forth to meet the Others in the Battle for the Dawn" (II.330). In a released *The Winds of Winter* chapter, the battle of Meereen will also begin at dawn. Someone says "A red dawn," and Barristan thinks, "A dragon dawn."

It seems likely Ser Arthur Dayne the Sword of the Morning and his legendary sword Dawn will have some place in the story. Though Ned Stark killed this Kingsguard hero just after Robert's Rebellion, his sword was famously unique. Many wonder if his blade, made from a comet, is meant to be Lightbringer. Dawn also symbolizes newness and youth as well as light, reminding fans that the young heroes like Bran may be crucial to the story.

Darkness

"Never fear the darkness, Bran. The strongest trees are rooted in the dark places of the earth. Darkness will be your cloak, your shield, your mother's milk. Darkness will make you strong," the three-eyed crow tells Bran Stark (V.450). Jaime dreams of going underground and discovering truth and honor in the person of Brienne. Bran emerges from the Stark crypts where he was safe to find himself in a world of well-lit violence and snow.

Darkness is not always evil – it can symbolize the fertility of fresh soil, or the underground world of spirit and growth as in the above passage. This lesson suggests that the war against eternal night may not be as Bran assumes – light and dark, night and day must exist in a balance. Melisandre likewise comments that shadows can only exist because of light. True darkness is safer.

Moon

The crescent moon, emblem of House Arryn, is a heraldic symbol of hope to greater honor (Mounet Lipp). Of course, with a motto of "As High as Honor," this is the quality the House prizes above all. Lysa Arryn's home is a moonlit reflection of herself – the

Godswood is dead, and icy white stone predominates. It's an empty place, "as high as honor" but vacant of love and loyalty. The place is feminized but also cast as murderous and cold with its infamous sky cells and moon door. The men treat the Eyrie with indifference and disdain, much as they treat the lady and her son. When Tyrion notes, "They say the Eyrie is impregnable," Bronn retorts, "Give me twenty good men and some climbing spikes and I'll pregnate the bitch" ("The Wolf and the Lion").

The moon is a feminine symbol, as Drogo calls Dany "Moon of my life." Daenerys walks into the lake under the moonlight in a ceremony to wash off the horse heart's blood in the books. The moon is magical and silvery, constantly changing, growing fatter and slimmer like a pregnant woman's belly. It also is fabled to be the origin of dragons:

> Doreah: A trader from Qarth told me that Dragons come from the moon.
> Daenerys Targaryen: The moon?
> Doreah: He told me the moon was an egg, khaleesi. That once there were two moons in the sky, but one wandered too close to the sun and it cracked from the heat. Out of it poured a thousand thousand dragons and they drank the sun's fire. ("The Kingsroad")

In another tale, it's the forging of the magical sword Lightbringer that cracked the moon: "Azor Ahai thrust the smoking sword through [his wife's] living heart. It is said that her cry of anguish and ecstasy left a crack across the face of the moon, but her blood and her soul and her strength and her courage all went into the steel" (II.115). Once again the magic of light and creation, together with women's mysteries creates the moon.

Ned Stark tells Arya of Sansa. "You may be as different as the sun and the moon, but the same blood flows through both your hearts. You need her, as she needs you" (I.223). Presumably red-headed Sansa, concerned with the men's world of tourneys and kingly power, is the sun, while quiet, crafty Arya, who still has her wolf magic, is the moon.

In the fifth book, John dreams of the moon – who possibly symbolizes someone trying to contact him.

> The white wolf raced through a black wood, beneath a pale cliff as tall as the sky. The moon ran with him.
> "Snow," the moon murmured. The wolf made no answer.
> "Snow," the moon called down again, cackling.
> "Snow," the moon insisted. The white wolf ran from it, racing toward the cave of night where the sun had hidden,
> "Snow." an icicle tumbled from a branch. The white wolf turned and bared its teeth. (V.46)

Daenerys has the most "moon magic" but characters like Bran or the three-eyed crow are possible as this moon messenger, or Jon may be foretelling something in the future.

Night

> Night gathers, and now my watch begins. It shall not end until my death. I shall take no wife, hold no lands, father no children. I shall wear no crowns and win no glory. I shall live and die at my post. I am the sword in the darkness. I am the watcher on the walls. I am the fire that burns against the cold, the light that brings the dawn, the horn that wakes the sleepers, the shield that guards the realms of men. I pledge my life and honor to the Night's Watch, for this night and all nights to come. (I.522)

In the Night's Watch oath, night is the force of evil, of the destructive wights and the night that lasted a generation in prehistory. The Red Priests agree, as Melisandre insists, "The night is dark and full of terrors." Both forces are resolved to fight the "war for the dawn" and defeat the forces of winter ... though this may turn out differently than they expect.

Just as there have been champions of the light, there have also been forces of night: The Night's King, a legendary Lord Commander of the Night's Watch, fell in love with a woman "with skin as white as the moon and eyes like blue stars," though "her skin was cold as ice" (III.762). With the Nightfort as his castle, he terrorized his subjects and sacrificed them to the White Walkers, as Craster does. He loved a wight and betrayed the Watch, until the King in the North killed him. It's said the king was in fact a Stark, brother to the King. It can be hoped that Bran and Jon won't reenact this legend.

Rains of Castamere

> Cersei: Ah, but you know the song "The Rains of Castamere"?
> Margaery: Of course. They play it so often here at court.
> Cersei: So you know the story of House Reyne of Castamere?
> Margaery: Not as well as you, I'm sure.
> Cersei: House Reyne was a powerful family. Very wealthy. The second wealthiest in Westeros. Aren't the Tyrells the second wealthiest family in Westeros now? Of course, ambitious climbers don't want to stop on the second highest rung. If only you could take that final step, you'd see further than all the rest. You'd be alone with nothing but blue sky above you. So Lord Reyne built a castle as grand as Casterly Rock. He gave his wife diamonds larger than any my mother ever wore. And finally one day, he rebelled against my father. Do you

know where House Reyne is now?
Margaery: Gone.
Cersei: Gone. A gentle word. Why not say slaughtered?
Every man, woman, and child put to the sword. I
remember seeing their bodies hanging high above the
gates of Casterly Rock. My father let them rot up there all
summer. It was a long summer. "And now the rains weep
o'er their halls, and not a soul to hear." If you ever call me
sister again, I'll have you strangled in your sleep.
("Second Sons")

This history of the Family of Reyne appears often in the series, as minstrels sing "The Rains of Castamere" often to flatter the Lannisters. In the book, most of the seven singers at Joffrey's wedding sing it – As Lady Olenna snarks, "I hope they play "Rains of Castamere." It's been ten minutes since I heard it last; I've forgotten how it goes" (III.826). On the show, Tywin has the greatsword of the Starks disassembled as the song echoes as the background music. Then Oberyn hears someone singing it on a brothel, identifies the man as a Lannister, and starts stabbing.

Nonetheless, the message about pride coming before a fall is one the Lannisters should heed as well. In the books, Prince Oberyn's daughter Obara remarks that she wants to drive her spear into Lord Tywin's belly. As she puts it, "I'll make him sing 'The Rains of Castamere' as I pull his bowels out and look for gold" (IV.33). It plays of the credits of the second episode, "The Lion and the Rose."

As the literal rain washes the Reynes' ancestral seat, the song makes a less-than-subtle pun. The episode of the Red Wedding is called "The Rains of Castamere," and the minstrels suddenly play the song before the Freys take their vengeance. It's also sung over the end to the credits.

Robb and his companions ride through heavy rain to reach the Freys, foreshadowing what's to come. "This is an evil rain," Catelyn says. "This rain beats us down. The banners hang limp and sodden, and the men huddle under their cloaks" (III.630). Rain is a masculine symbol, associating with the sky god fertilizing the earth. As such, the Reynes of Castamere are a sign of male pride, struggling against the next rung of the hierarchy and being destroyed.

The other significant rain (aside from storms, which have a separate entry) is Davos's holdings. Davos is "Lord of the Rainwood, Admiral of the Narrow Sea, and Hand of the King [Stannis]." His wife and younger sons are at Cape Wrath, in the castle of Rainwood. With a new player attacking the area in released chapters from book six, Davos may have a great conflict ahead.

Smoke

The Smoking Sea surrounds Old Valyria, recalling the destruction when Old Valyria fell. Some believe it was a volcano, others insist on fire magic, dragons, or sorcerous experiments. Either way, nothing remains but the smoke-filled ruins, and their heirs, the Targaryens.

In recent times, there is the prophecy, "Azor Ahai shall be born again amidst smoke and salt to wake dragons out of stone." Melisandre's fires produce smoke and shadows, which she uses for her magic. Daenerys's funeral pyres also offer clouds of smoke, as did the destruction surrounding her birth. Smoke is known as a combination of air and fire. Thus it is the force of flying, flaming dragons, the antithesis of earth and water. In alchemy, smoke symbolizes the soul leaving the body (Cirlot 300). Daenerys and her other dragonriders (whoever they are) must embark on a spiritual journey as well as a literal one. Smoke and ashes suggest ruin and mourning, while the grey color offers an ambiguity – smoke can be a blessing or destruction:

> Smoke has come to suggest vanity and all that is fleeting because it rises into the air only to disappear. Symbolically, it is a reminder of the shortness of this life and the futility of seeking earthly glory. The anger and wrath of God were ofttimes indicated by smoke. "O God, why hast Thou cast us off for ever? Why doth Thine anger smoke against the sheep of Thy pasture?" [Psalm 73:1]. (Ferguson 44)

Thus the savior of Westeros will rise from evanescence and destruction to save the world with the power of light and a flaming sword.

Spring

The final book "A Dream of Spring" suggests the season will bring rejuvenation and rebirth to the world, along with an end to the terrible winter. Spring is traditionally a time of happiness, of young love and young animals, of fresh vegetables and new-tilled spoil. Starvation is over, and light and life return to the world.

Martin's series appears to stretch from Summer through Autumn and Winter to Spring once more. In a popular life stages metaphor, autumn and winter symbolize maturity, while spring is childhood and summer is youth. Certainly the characters age from innocent youths like Arya, Bran, and Daenerys into experienced warriors. The final season of spring foretells children being born and new dynasties created, with the birth of a new era for Westeros.

Spring is also a time for comedy, and Dunk and Egg, short story protagonists who have not yet hatched into heroes or leaders, set forth in the spring, with Dunk admittedly none-too-bright and none-too-skilled at jousting, while his wisecracking sidekick has brains for the two of them. "The characters of Dunk and Egg, in fact, seem precisely crafted to serve as comic alternatives to the more serious-minded events of the main series" (Westfahl 61).

In the Dunk and Egg stories, the symbolism of spring and freshness is not always positive. Many characters are said to have "died in the Spring," the spring sickness that claimed thousands of lives, royal and commoner.

A Song of Ice and Fire has many mentions of the tournament in "the Year of the False Spring" when Prince Rhaegar crowned Lyanna Stark Queen of Love and Beauty instead of his own wife and began the troubles that led to the Targaryens' downfall. While spring suggests hope and renewal, a false spring is false hope, leading to destruction and despair. Similarly, Tyrion pictures Tysha and the "false spring of their marriage" (V.21).

Storms
When Bran dreams of his family, he thinks, "A storm was gathering ahead of them, a vast dark roaring lashed by lightning, but somehow they could not see it" (I.136-137). Melisandre warns Jon, "I have seen you in the storm, hard-pressed, with enemies on every side. You have so many enemies. Shall I tell you their names?" (V.59). As such, the storm becomes a

metaphor for violence and war. In the short story "The Mystery Knight" on the eve of a rebellion, someone says, "A few drops of rain and all the bold lords go squealing for shelter. What will they do when the real storm breaks, I wonder" (714).

The Stormlands, one of the Seven Kingdoms, are the ancestral holding of House Baratheon, House of three kings in the War of the Five Kings (if Joffrey is counted as well as Stannis and Renly). They were also the driving force of Robert's Rebellion. In the series, there are battles in the Stormlands several times, and Stannis unleashes a shadow creature there in the second book. It's clearly a place of battle.

Likewise, the bastards named Storm are a source of contention, as Edric Storm from the books takes Gendry's plot in "Second Sons" and is nearly sacrificed to the Lord of Light. There's also Beric Dondarrion, who preys on knights throughout the Riverlands as a force of violence and chaos, with forked purple lightning on a black field for his sigil.

The storm represents creativity – a mixture between elements leading to newness. The storm god is Zeus, Thor, Bel, Donar, or Peroun, a masculine figure of great strength and power (Cirlot 315). Thus the chosen one, like Daenerys Stormborn, will be created from the chaos and bring rejuvenation to the world.

Summer

Summer is the time of warmth, pleasantness, and happiness, when the series starts. It's also a time of unrealistic happiness and naïve existence. "Within Sansa's songs, all knights are gallant, maids are always beautiful, the season is always summer, and honor always rules" (Goguen 212). Of course, as Ned warns his family, "Winter is Coming." Catelyn calls Renly's men the "knights of summer," inexperienced in real war. Thus summer, innocence and youthfulness, fades quickly as war falls upon everyone. Ned says, "Summer will end soon enough and childhood as well" (I.67). Bran and Arya are children of summer, but as Ned says, "Now the winter is truly coming" (I.222). Alliser Thorne tells the recruits, "You are boys still, green and stinking of summer, and when the winter comes, you will die like flies" (I.444). Tyrion has lived through many summers, the latest of which has lasted ten years. The next winter will be terrible. Commander Mormont asks him how many he's seen:

> He shrugged. "Eight, nine. I misremember."
> "And all of them short."
> "As you say, my lord." He had been born in the dead of winter, a terrible cruel one that the maesters said had lasted near three years, but Tyrion's earliest memories were of spring.
> "When I was a boy, it was said that a long summer always meant a long winter to come. This summer has lasted nine years, Tyrion, and a tenth will soon be upon us. Think on that."
> "When I was a boy," Tyrion replied, "my wet nurse told me that one day, if men were good, the gods would give the world a summer without ending. Perhaps we've been better than we thought, and the Great Summer is finally at hand." He grinned.
> The Lord Commander did not seem amused. "You are not fool enough to believe that, my lord. Already the days grow shorter. There can be no mistake, Aemon has had letters from the Citadel, findings in accord with his own. The end of summer stares us in the face." (I.207-208)

Patchface, Stannis's jester, makes an odd rhyme which may or may not have a touch of prophecy: "It is always summer under the sea. The merwives wear nennymoans in their hair and weave gowns of silver seaweed. I know, I know, oh, oh, oh" (II.6). It's unclear whether mermaids actually exist, or whether peace or magic to fight the Others truly waits below the deeps. If the girl in a silver gown with poisonous creatures in her hair is Sansa (this is how she dresses for the book's Purple Wedding), then it is "always summer" in King's Landing – it may be safe from the Others. Perhaps that's why the old kings in Winterfell have steel swords on their crypts to "prevent them from walking."

Summerhall was a Targaryen home, where many inexperienced princes lived, sheltered and peaceful. The name is associated with a great tragedy, however, as many royal residents burned to death apparently trying to awaken dragons. Youthful folly seems central here.

> Summerhall is another mysterious disaster, happening at the time of Prince Rhaegar's birth and costing him his great-grandfather. King Aegon V sought to create a hot enough fire to hatch the petrified dragon eggs, but instead burned down himself and several family members in an intense conflagration. Ser Barristan recalls Summerhall as an incident of "sorcery, fire, and grief" (V:875). Were the Valyrians attempting a similar experiment? (Frankel, *Winter is Coming*)

Summer as a time of warmth and innocence seems reflected in the Summer Islanders from the Summer Sea, who sing and practice free love while drinking rum and eating fruit. Tyrion hires the ship the Summer's Dream while at the height of his power to condemn treacherous Janos Slynt to the Wall. Of course, he loses that power soon after.

Bran names his wolf Summer, suggesting the magic he will need to combat the coming winter and the Others. As described in Martin's Dunk and Egg, "The summers have been shorter since the last dragon died, and the winters longer and crueler" ("The Hedge Knight," 607). It's possible the Targaryens and their dragon powers are holding back the winter merely by living and ruling. If so, Daenerys's return will help turn the tide.

Sun

House Martell, who rule from Sunspear in the scorching desert of Dorne, bear a sun sigil. In heraldry, the sun, most often depicted in its splendor, represents "Power, glory, illumination, vitality, and the source of life on earth" (Mounet Lipp). The sun is a masculine symbol and represents the pinnacle of spiritual development and human achievement. Quentyn and Oberyn fall short, but other leaders of Dorne may have a great victory or find enlightenment through the course of the series. It should also be mentioned that their sigil is technically a "red star," and various Martells bleed and die through the series. Thus the prophecy of "When the red star bleeds and the darkness gathers, Azor Ahai shall be born again amidst smoke and salt" could apply to them (the red comet is a more obvious choice, of course).

The sun is unchanging and constant, unlike the moon. It purifies, and on the positive side, signifies "glory, spirituality, and illumination." On the negative side, it is vanity and unrealistic idealism (Cirlot 230). Oberyn Martell suffers heavily from these latter two, while it may be hoped his daughters will bring the former qualities to Westeros someday.

Stannis's sword of light symbolizes the sun, as Jon comments that "It glows like it had a piece of sun inside it" and thinks later, "The sword glowed red and yellow and orange, alive with light. Jon had seen the show before but not like this, never before like this. Lightbringer was the sun made steel" (V.138-138). However, he appears to be a false hero of destiny, just as is Lightbringer is false – cold to the touch and quenched only in burning statues of gods he never truly worshipped.

The Karstark motto is "The Sun of Winter" with a white sunburst on black. Likewise, the pirate Salladhor Saan's shirts are embroidered with sunbursts on the show. Jaime and Cersei are often compared with the sun in their golden beauty. Of course, Jaime in the early seasons is the epitome of privilege in the masculine hierarchy of King's Landing and Cersei is at its head through her marriage to the king. They all fall short of their goals. Drogo, Daenerys's "sun and stars" falls in battle early – the symbolism suggests the patriarchy as sun will fall and Daenerys will rise. This pattern follows with the Karstarks and Dorne, as their women are left to rule their houses. Brienne's sigil of House Tarth is yellow suns on rose quartered with white crescents on azure. As a female knight, a character caught symbolically and literally between sun and moon, she may conquer the patriarchy as well.

Winter

Old Nan begins the book and show by telling of the ancient past, with an endless winter and the terrible Others:

> Oh, my sweet summer child. What do you know about fear? Fear is for the winter when the snows fall a hundred feet deep. Fear is for the long nights when the sun hides for years, and children are born and live and die, all in darkness. That is the time for fear, my little lord; when the white walkers move through the woods.
>
> Thousands of years ago there came a night that lasted a generation. Kings froze to death in their castles, same as the shepherds in their huts, and women smothered their babies rather than see them starve, and wept and felt their tears freeze on their cheeks. So is this the sort of story that you like? In that darkness the white walkers came for the first time. They swept through cities and kingdoms, riding their dead horses, hunting with their packs of pale spiders big as hounds. ("Winter is Coming")

Now that everyone has forgotten the lore, winter is coming. Unfortunately viewers never hear the end of Old Nan's tale. Describing the First Men, Jon says, "I think they were afraid. I think they came here [to Westeros] to get away from something. I don't think it worked" ("The Ghost of Harrenhal"). Did the ice magic follow them from another place?

In the book, the story continues a bit longer: the last hero of the First Men set out to find the children of the forest, whose ancient magics could restore mankind's lost wisdom. He left with his sword, a dog, his horse, and twelve companions. When only he was left, the Others attacked ... and then the tale is interrupted. As Bran travels North with his wolf and a few companions, he seems to echo the hero of this tale.

> When Bran and Rickon leave Maester Luwin in the
> Godswood at season two's end, six of them set out –
> exactly half of twelve, just as half of Bran is left to be a
> hero. Bran, Rickon, Hodor, Osha, Jojen, and Meera walk
> into the forest (in the book, these last two children were
> staying at Winterfell and escaped with the Stark boys). If
> one adds the people, from guides to fellow travelers, the
> children find on the way North, the number reaches
> exactly twelve companions, at least for a night here and
> there. As Bran and his wolf travel steadily north, his story
> echoes the Last Hero's. He's even a descendent of the
> First Men, as all Northmen are. On his hero-quest, it's
> clear that Bran will descend into the darkest place all
> alone, as the Last Hero once did. There, he will confront
> the Other beyond the curtain, the one he has seen in his
> dreams. (Frankel, *Winning the Game* 113-114)

Bran is clearly on a quest to battle the winter, with his wolf that he names Summer after waking from his dream:

> North and north and north he looked, to the curtain of
> light at the end of the world, and then beyond that
> curtain. He looked deep into the heart of winter, and then
> he cried out, afraid, and the heat of his tears burned his
> cheeks.
> Now you know, the crow whispered as it sat on his
> shoulder, now you know why you must live.
> "Why?" Bran said, not understanding, falling, falling.
> Because winter is coming. (I.136-137)

It arrives by the sixth book, *The Winds of Winter.*

COLORS

Black and White

Black and white as a combination symbolize starkness, truth, and purity of life. They offer the absolute dichotomy of truth and falsehood, right and wrong. Ned Stark judges Gregor Clegane and sentences him in "black and white and grey, all the shades of truth" (I.464). The Karstarks' colors are black and white, and they prove uncompromising as Lord Karstark kills the innocent Lannister squires in payment for his sons' deaths. Robb responds with black and white justice and executes him. While Melisandre doesn't wear black and white, she and Stannis also live in this polarized world – him with justice, her with her religion. There can be no compromise. Likewise, Maisie Williams (Arya) notes of her character: "Everything in her world is black and white. She finds it weird how people can say 'maybe'" (Cogman 58).

She finds her way to the House of Black and White: the house of death. There is no pretense, no shading. People come to die, and they do. In the House of Black and White "we've left behind traditional ideas of good and evil" (Jacoby, "No One Dances the Water Dance" 247). Nonetheless, there is an incontrovertible code, mostly about being selfless and only acting on behalf of others. One must be invisible, clever, hyper-aware, but also a tool for others to use. The doors of the House of Black and White are ebony and weirwood.

> At the top she found a set of carved wooden doors twelve feet high. The left-hand door was made of weirwood pale as bone, the right of gleaming ebony. In their center was a carved moon face; ebony on the weirwood side, weirwood on the ebony. The look reminded her somehow of the heart tree in the godswood at Winterfell. The doors are watching me, she thought. (IV.95)

There are ebony and weirwood doors in the House of the Undying as well, "the black and white grains swirling and twisting in strange interwoven patterns" (II.703).

The Night's Watch wear black. Their oath suggests they're sworn to combat the pale Others, so the black is a form of defiance. Their colors stand out impractically against the white snow, suggesting they're a force of boldness, rather than hiding.

The Kingsguard wear white cloaks and their tower is completely white:

> The White Book sat on a white table in a white room. The room was round, its walls of whitewashed stone hung with white woolen tapestries. It formed the first floor of White Sword Tower, a slender structure of four stories

> built into an angle of the castle wall overlooking the bay. The undercroft held arms and armor, the second and third floors the small spare sleeping cells of the six brothers of the Kingsguard. (III.912)

Here it symbolizes their pure chastity (ironically like the Black Brothers) and humility – knights in both give up their family colors and shields in order to serve. It's unclear whether the White Cloaks and Black Brothers will end up uniting in some way, or simply continue to selflessly protect the kingdom from south and north.

Black

Among knights, "black is associated with sin, penitence, the withdrawal of the recluse, the hidden, rebirth in seclusion, and sorrow" (Cirlot 171). The Black Brothers echo much of this. Likewise, the Targaryen red echoes their motto of "fire and blood," while their black sigils suggest smoke or darkness. Black means constancy and strength but also grief in heraldry. The Targaryens and Black Brothers constantly encounter all three. Likewise, the black stag of the Baratheons signals constancy as stubbornness in Robert and his brothers, who fall to grief one by one. The black banner of the Ironmen reflects similar traits among the Greyjoys. The Cleganes with their three black dogs certainly cause and feel intense grief (or at least the Hound does). Drogon, the black dragon, may also represent this unwavering strength and grief for Daenerys.

Blue

The Tullys and Arryns share the blue of truth and loyalty, according to the dictates of heraldry.

Ironically, Lysa Arryn, the one character of both houses, bases her life around severe lies. She is also remarkably disloyal, turning her back on father, sister, and nephews in their dire need. The Blackfish, despite the color in his name, lives up far better to Tully and Arryn values.

The characters most seen wearing blue are Daenerys and Catelyn. Blue, the color of sky and sea, represents divinity. "Blue has also come to symbolize purity: Christians associate it with the Virgin Mary, and it is the Roman Catholic liturgical color used on her feast days" (Shepherd 344). She is always pictured as wearing a blue gown with red scarf or cloak. Other maternal characters are notable for their blue imagery. Some septas wear blue robes. Lady Olenna and Margaery wear sky blue at times, linking the two women together and emphasizing their status as past and future mothers. Ned Stark dreams of Lyanna in a storm of blue rose petals, associating her with ice and also motherhood – she may have had a child with the Targaryen prince who stole her away. Stannis's Queen Selyse comes from House Florent of Brightwater, whose banner is a red fox in a circle of blue flowers. Thus Selyse, Lysa, and Catelyn, all mothers, wives, and matriarchs of their houses before all, combine red and blue in their house colors, like Mary, mother of Jesus.

Blue can also represent corrupting magic: the magicians of Qarth drink shade of the evening until their lips turn blue. The Others are known for shining blue eyes. Daenerys dreams in the House of the Undying and appears to see Westeros:

A long stone table filled this room. Above it floated a

126

> human heart, swollen and blue with corruption, yet still
> alive. It beat, a deep ponderous throb of sound, and each
> pulse sent out a wash of indigo light. The figures around
> the table were no more than blue shadows. (II.704)

The five kings are corrupt, and the magic of the Others is coming to overwhelm Westeros. Daenerys must act, before it is too late.

Brown

The humblest orders of monks wear brown, suggesting their modest roles. Certainly, many houses in the book have brown sigils. The color generally signifies humility or a renunciation of the world, so it's unsurprising none of the Great Houses use it. By contrast, Missandei wears pale brown, while Barristan and Ser Jorah wear dark brown in season four. On the show, Brienne's armor is textured with lines like wheat and pale brown in color, suggesting her humility as she fights for the good of Westeros. In season three, Jaime wears muddy brown with a tattered sling, emphasizing his degrading situation. The rags have an open weave like a peasant's.

The Selmy arms are three stalks of wheat on a brown field, emphasizing Barristan's humble nature. Ser Barristan, possibly the most selfless character of the series, truly does fight for the good of the realm beyond his personal honor or inclination. He defends Prince Rhaegar Targaryen and nearly dies of it, then leads the Kingsguard under King Robert in order to bring peace to the realm under a just ruler, a decision that takes priority over Targaryen loyalty. He tells Daenerys later that her brother Viserys seemed to have a taint of madness, so Barristan could not support him. When Joffrey dismisses him, Barristan haughtily refuses honorable retirement and finds Daenerys. In the book, he observes her for some time before confessing his identity to her – he's determined to serve the best person for Westeros. When Daenerys threatens to demote Barristan to her cook, he accepts with "quiet dignity," saying, "I can bake apples and boil beef as well as any man, and I've roasted many a duck over a campfire" (III.988). If the service is honorable, it need not fit his station.

Gold

In heraldry, gold "signifies glory, faith, constancy, and wisdom" (Shepherd 343). Targaryen hair is silver and gold in the books, emphasizing their royal birthright. The Lannisters are similarly born to wealth with shining golden hair. The Baratheon or Lannister gold sigils symbolize kingly generosity and elevation of the mind. Certainly Robert, the patriarch of the Baratheons, is known for royal generosity, though all the Baratheons, from his brothers to his alleged sons, fail to find the mental elevation essential to kingship. The Lannisters have the most gold of anyone and famously "pay their debts" though they call them in as well. The Tyrells with their golden rose are more generous, but their elevation of the mind has not yet been seen.

Of course, gold can also suggest vicious greed. Xaro in season two wears cloth of gold leaves embroidered with bees, emphasizing his golden wealth. "The precious metal, gold, is used as the symbol of pure light, the heavenly element in which God lives. It is also used as a symbol of worldly wealth and idolatry" (Ferguson 42). While it can signify worthy kingship, it more often suggests those who steal gold coins or require extensive bribes. Joffrey marries in cloth of gold, suggesting pride and ostentation. Sansa's wedding gown on the show is elaborate swirls and flowers against a pale gold. She is not a Lannister, but they are trying to make her a softer imitation of one.

Kingship can be destructive as well – those who play the Game of Thrones often die of it. Khal Drogo crowns Viserys with melted gold, killing him with the symbol he most covets. The Blackfyres, rebellious Targaryen descendants in exile, dip the skulls of their dead in gold, vowing to bring them all home. It seems clear they'll play a part in the war to come. A decade before book five's release, Martin wrote, "The Golden Company is the largest and most famous, founded by one of Aegon the Unworthy's bastards. You won't meet them until *A Dance With Dragons*" ("So Spake Martin" C91, P180). It seems more claimants will be battling for the throne.

Green

Some of the tiny, magical children of the forest reputedly had greensight. Their wise men were called Greenseers. "The children of the forest were the first people, small as children, dark and beautiful....They worshipped the old gods and their wisemen, the greenseers, carved the faces that keep watch in the weirwoods" (I.736-37).

"Only one man in a thousand is born a skinchanger," the three-eyed crow tells Bran, "And only one skinchanger in a thousand can be a greenseer" (V.451). It's suggested that Jon, Arya, and possibly the other Starks are shapechangers with animal bonds. There are several wargs among the Wildlings. Bran appears the only greenseer. The concept of a greenseer reflects the Green Man from ancient Britain, an ancient spirit of life and growth. It also makes sense that Bran's power to fight the ice is a green power – that of summer and growing things. "Green is the color of nature, life, renewal, and earth" (Shepherd 343). In Christian lore, it represents hope.

Crannogmen keep many of the old ways, and Howland Reed goes to commune with the children on the mysterious Isle of Faces. Jojen Reed, his son, has greensight and also unnaturally green eyes. Arya, Bran, and the Reeds wear greenish brownish forest colors as they blend among the trees, and in the book, Jojen Reed is all in green. All these characters fight with the power of woods and nature, traveling unseen.

Heraldic green, seen in the Tyrell colors, represents hope, joy, beauty, and loyalty in love. While her presence tends to evoke all these things, Lady Margaery can hardly be regarded as "loyal" to her beloveds, of whom there are many. Renly, allied with House Tyrell, takes a standard of a golden stag on a field of green. He and his companions are certainly "green knights" – "The green knight is the pre-knight, the squire, the apprentice sworn to knighthood" (Cirlot 171). While Ser Loras is unfailingly loyal to Renly, in his life and after his death in the books, this does little to help Renly, slain in the flower of his life.

Grey

Gray signifies ashes, humility, and mourning, as well as the mortality of the body and the immortality of the soul. All this is seen in the grey-dressed Silent Sisters who never speak, only tend the dead. The Maesters, mediators between life and death, magic and science, wear grey as well. Lady Stoneheart, trapped between a sort of unlife and the grave, wears grey. Grey Worm is the humblest of Daenerys's inner circle, and Melisandre calls Davos "A grey man, neither black nor white, but partaking of both" (II.620). On the show, Stark soldiers wear grey and brown. Talisa often wears grey, suggesting a practical, simple nature rather than pride.

While Grey Wind is named for his swiftness and proud Winterfell coloring, his name may also hint at mourning as he and Robb are killed. Wildlings wear grey as they're torn apart by the White Walkers. They are neither friend nor foe to those of Westeros as the great enemy attacks and they're caught between forces of black and white.

Orange

The ancient Martells of old used a spear as their emblem, while conquering queen Nymeria and her people the Rhoynar used the sun as theirs. When Nymeria wed King Mors Martell, they combined these into a gold spear piercing a red sun on an orange field. Their words are "Unbowed, Unbent, Unbroken." Prince Oberyn and his paramour Ellaria dress in yellow and orange with suns, displaying their colors at court both literally and metaphorically. Orange represents worthy ambition. As revealed in the later books, Dorne has long-term plans for the succession, even while staying out of the immediate war. As the family of the late Targaryen queen, Daenerys's sister-in-law, their vengeance could indeed be termed "worthy," though their ambition may only prolong the civil war.

Pink

Pink suggests femininity and also sensuality, because it's similar to flesh tones. Shae and Sansa wear some pink. Obviously, Shae is a sex object by her choice and Tyrion's, while Sansa is fought over as a marriage pawn. Margaery wears pink on occasion as well. Pink can also suggest grace, perfect happiness, gentility, and admiration, things all three ladies strive for.

Daenerys's dresses when she meets and marries Drogo on the show are a pale flesh tone. The "viewing dress is essentially designed to make her look good naked, as Drogo's come by to see the goods, basically," notes costume designer Michelle Clapton (Cogman 158). Her wedding dress is nearly as transparent, emphasizing her near-nakedness and vulnerability. It wraps around, inviting Drogo to unwrap it. When she walks into the pyre, Daenerys burns in it, shedding her life with Drogo and wearing stronger colors thereafter.

Purple

In Europe, purple was an extremely rare and costly dye made from murex and purpura mollusks; thus it was worn only by the exceedingly rich. In time, laws were passed that only royalty could wear it. Daenerys has a purple audience chamber in Meereen in the books, and she wears purple and silver there. She meets Drogo in a purple gown, emphasizing her royal birthright. Her purple Targaryen eyes stress her hereditary right to rule. (Prince Rhaegar and Aegon V had these eyes, suggesting their own worthiness, while other weaker Targaryens like Viserys and book five's Aegon have eyes of lighter purple).

The Purple Wedding is so-nicknamed by fans because of all its royal ostentation as well as its dark, rich wine. Sansa wears a very significant hairnet of dark amethysts to it, though it's a purple drop necklace on the show. Purple suggests the rarity of the gems but also a crimson tinge of dark blood. Similar stones are seen in Braavos and in the chamber of Cressen, the maester who poisons Melisandre and himself in season two:

> His chambers seemed dim and gloomy after the brightness of the morning. With fumbling hands, the old man lit a candle and carried it to the workroom beneath the rookery stair, where his ointments, potions, and medicines stood neatly on their shelves. On the bottom shelf behind a row of salves in squat clay jars he found a vial of indigo glass, no larger than his little finger. It rattled when he shook it. Cressen blew away a layer of dust and carried it back to his table. Collapsing into his chair, he pulled the stopper and spilled out the vial's contents. A dozen crystals, no larger than seeds, rattled across the parchment he'd been reading. They shone like jewels in the candlelight, so purple that the maester found himself thinking that he had never truly seen the color before.
>
> The chain around his throat felt very heavy. He touched one of the crystals lightly with the tip of his little finger. Such a small thing to hold the power of life and death. It was made from a certain plant that grew only on the islands of the Jade Sea, half a world away. The leaves had to be aged, and soaked in a wash of limes and sugar water and certain rare spices from the Summer Isles. Afterward they could be discarded, but the potion must be thickened with ash and allowed to

crystallize. The process was slow and difficult, the necessaries costly and hard to acquire. The alchemists of Lys knew the way of it, though, and the Faceless Men of Braavos... and the maesters of his order as well, though it was not something talked about beyond the walls of the Citadel. All the world knew that a maester forged his silver link when he learned the art of healing-but the world preferred to forget that men who knew how to heal also knew how to kill. Cressen no longer recalled the name the Asshaii gave the leaf, or the Lysene poisoners the crystal. In the Citadel, it was simply called the strangler. Dissolved in wine, it would make the muscles of a man's throat clench tighter than any fist, shutting off his windpipe. They said a victim's face turned as purple as the little crystal seed from which his death was grown, but so too did a man choking on a morsel of food. (II.21) .

Rainbow

The Warrior's Sons, militant arm of the New Gods' religion, have rainbow cloaks and a rainbow sword on their standard, mirroring the rainbow crystals in the High Septon's crown. Certainly the rainbow has seven colors, and it's an unsubtle burst of color, a sign of strength. In today's world, the rainbow can be a similarly religious symbol.

> The rainbow is a symbol of union and, because it appeared after the Flood, it is also the symbol of pardon and of the reconciliation given to the human race by God. In art, the rainbow is used as the Lord's throne, and in representations of the Last Judgment, Christ is often seated upon it. "...behold, a throne was set in Heaven, and one sat on the throne...and there was a rainbow round about the throne." [Apoc. 4:2-3]. (Ferguson 43)

Renly's Rainbow Guard appears to evoke similar imagery of strength in the Seven, though it's possible the "best dressed man in King's Landing" is simply eager to be surrounded by color.

Red

Red in heraldry represents martyrdom and a warrior's courage. Certainly, the Tullys, Lannisters, and Targaryens all lose enormous amounts of blood in the war of the Five Kings, and Robert's Rebellion, which preceded it. By contrast, war does not touch the cold blue and white Eyrie or fertile green and gold Reach. Dorne, represented by a red sun, may have a great deal more violence in their future.

Sansa and Margaery are cloaked in crimson at their ominous book three weddings, as is Lord Edmure's bride at the Red Wedding. Sansa's loyal fool Ser Dontos wears his surcoat of red and pink bars with three golden crowns in the books, and he's murdered in it. In the book, Viserys is executed in red Targaryen silks. On the show, Varys and Cersei wear red to Ned's execution. The throne room during Joffrey's rule is filled with banners of crimson, black, and gold and dramatic braziers that turn the light red.

The Glovers, with a red shield, are treated terribly in the books: Ethan Glover, companion to Brandon Stark, is killed by the Mad King. Asha captures Lady Sybella of Deepwood Mott and takes her and her children hostage, while her husband Galbart Glover fights for Robb Stark.

The Boltons' flayed man on pink is even less subtle, as is the red seven-pointed star of the Poor Fellows, another military arm of the Faith. The red star dates back to the Andal Invasion when zealous warriors carved actual seven-pointed stars into their chests. All this dramatic red serves to underscore the blood and violence of the show.

Silver

White and silver, the Stark colors, both represent sincerity, wisdom, innocence, peace and joy in heraldry. These qualities are scattered among the Stark children as they travel from innocence to wisdom and seek peace and joy on the other side of the war. Ned, of course, represents sincerity and honor, and his children mirror his values.

Because of its whiteness and precious quality, silver has become the symbol of purity and chastity. Psalm 11:7 states: "The words of the Lord are pure words: as silver tried in a furnace of earth, purified seven times," thus connecting silver with eloquence. It is often a feminine symbol, linked with moon magic. Daenerys receives a beautiful silver horse, as mystical and breathtaking as her own silver hair. She may fight with a mystical silver sword before the series ends.

SYMBOLS OF ICE AND FIRE

White and Ice

Martin comments, "What lies really north in my books – we haven't explored that yet, but we will in the last two books." He adds, "You're definitely going to see more of the Others" (Roberts). They are clearly the force of Ice in the world, as dragons are the force of fire. Yet there are other powers of Ice.

The Wall was built by heroes of Westeros to combat the Others. As such, it's a force of salvation and protection. Ice symbolizes a rigidness, and the death of potential as water is rendered immobile. Still, this can have positive associations with unyielding strength.

The mysterious wight Coldhands seems benevolent, though it's unclear why that is. The force of the Old Gods, made of red and white in equal balance as their magic appears in the weirwoods, may be powering him. It's also unclear what he is: is he a wight emissary from the Other, not so bad as assumed? Did the Children of the Forest rescue him from his transformation?

Characters of ice and cold include Jon Snow and his Stark siblings, Northerners like the Mormonts, and all the Wildlings and Black Brothers. The colors are gray, silver, and especially white, the color of ice itself. Winterfell is a place of paleness as "All the color had been leached from Winterfell until only grey and white remained" (V.489). Blue with blue-eyed wights and Lyanna's blue roses suggest cold and the North as well.

Weapons of ice include the Others' icicle blades and the Horn of Winter that is rumored to threaten the Wall itself. Jon's Longclaw is a northern sword of bear and wolf, though Ned Stark's Ice has become a pair of southern Lannister blades.

Red and Fire

In alchemy, fire is a tool of transmutation. While it can be used for good or evil, it often represents a battle and victory against the darkness. "To pass through the fire is symbolic of transcending the human condition" (Cirlot 106). By doing so, Daenerys asserts her status as more divine than mortal, achieving a new status for herself as a queen of dragons, wielder of ancient magics. On the show, Quaithe calls the dragons "fire made flesh. And fire is power" (2.5).

Daenerys has dragon dreams of rising from the flames as she becomes more powerful.

> She closed her eyes and whimpered. As if in answer, there was a hideous ripping sound and the crackling of some great fire. When she looked again Viserys was gone, great columns of flame rose all around, and in the midst of them was the dragon. It turned its great head slowly. When its molten eyes found hers, she woke, shaking and covered with a fine sweat. (I.101)

> There was only her and the dragon. Its scales were black as night, wet and slick with blood. Her blood, Dany sensed. Its eyes were pools of molten magma, and when it opened its mouth, the flame came roaring out in a hot jet. She could hear it singing to her. She opened her arms to the fire, embraced it, let it swallow her whole, let it cleanse her cleanse her and temper her and scour her clean. She could feel her flesh sear and blacken and slough away, could feel her blood boil and turn to steam, and yet there was no pain. She felt strong and new and fierce. (I.228)

Prophecy dictates that Daenerys must light "three fires ... one for life and one for death and one to love" (II.515). The first enabled her three dragons to live, recreating herself as Mother of Dragons through the power of fire. The others will transform her as well.

Other heroes share in the fire symbolism. Jon dreams of fighting with a blade that "burned red in his fist" (V.769) and Melisandre, staring into her flames, thinks, "I pray for a glimpse of Azor Ahai, and R'hllor shows me only [Jon] Snow" (V.408), suggesting he may be the chosen one who will create Lightbringer, sword of the Lord of Light. Burned by fire, he discovers how to kill a wight, and sets himself as the enemy of the ice.

"Fire and flames are symbolic of both martyrdom and religious fervor" (Ferguson 42). R'hllor's priests call him "the Heart of Fire, the God of Flame and Shadow," and pray he will save them from the Other and his darkness (II.20). His priestess, Melisandre, has copper colored hair and, in the books, red eyes. "Ygritte had been kissed by fire; the red priestess *was* fire, and her hair was blood and flame" (V.52). Thoros of Myr, Moqorro, and Quaithe are other red priests, and all of them attach themselves to those in power.

There are many characters associated with fire: all of the Targaryens were born to a family of "fire and blood" as well as dragons. The princes and princesses of Dorne dwell in a land of hot deserts and hot tempers with a sigil of red and orange. There's the Lannisters, marked by gold and red. Their words, "Hear me Roar," might apply to fire as well as to lions. The Hound is marked by fire, though it terrifies him. As Arya says, "I knew fear when I saw it in you. You're afraid of fire. When Beric's sword went up in flame, you looked like a scared little girl. And I know why, too. I heard what your brother did to you. Pressed your face to the fire like you're a nice juicy mutton chop" ("The Rains of Castamere").

Weapons of fire include the horn that controls dragons and blisters lungs. Dragons themselves are a weapon of fire. Dragon fire was used to create "dragonsteel," (likely Valyrian steel) and may have created dragonglass, obsidian. Swords of fire include the fabled Lightbringer and Dawn, Brightroar (the lost sword of House Lannister), and Targaryen swords Blackfyre and Dark Sister. Wildfire appears to be a chemical substitute for dragons. As characters note, "After the dragons died, wildfire was the key to Targaryen power ... the substance is fire given form" (2.5).

Fire can also be a metaphor for violence and destruction. "Red is the color of fire and blood, hence its association with anger and aggression, and war deities such as Ares and Ogun" (Shepherd 343). Many villages are torched, and innocents killed by fire in the series.

> The red priest squatted down beside her. "My lady," he said, "the Lord granted me a view of Riverrun. An island in a sea of fire, it seemed. The flames were leaping lions with long crimson claws. And how they roared! A sea of Lannisters, my lady. Riverrun will soon come under attack." (III.497)

The sky is always red above Old Valyria, and those who look on that land are doomed. In the ancient past, every hill for 500 miles exploded, filling the sky with fire and killing even the dragons. "Red clouds rained down dragonglass and the black blood of demons" (V.446). The Lands of the Long Summer were blighted and withered. With "smoking ruins" (I.374) by the Smoking Sea (III.98), and the shattered peninsula that was once a mighty empire, it appears the cataclysm was a volcanic eruption.

Hardhome, the only Wildling town, was also burned to cinders, in a fire so hot it could be seen from the Wall. It's unclear whether this was the work of volcanoes, magic, or the firewyrms that could bore through soil and stone (IV.321). Any of these may be the counter to the Endless Winter that approaches.

Ice and Fire

Prince Rhaegar says of his baby son, "He is the prince that was promised, and his is the song of ice and fire" (II.701). In the House of the Undying, his sister

Daenerys hears the puzzling words, "the shape of shadows ... morrows not yet made .... drink from the cup of ice ... drink from the cup of fire" (II.705). Daenerys dreams of fighting ice with her fire in a prophetic vision that may come true:

> That night she dreamt that she was Rhaegar, riding to the Trident. But she was mounted on a dragon, not a horse. When she saw the Usurper's rebel host across the river they were armored all in ice, but she bathed them in dragonfire and they melted away like dew and turned the Trident into a torrent. Some small part of her knew that she was dreaming, but another part exulted. *This is how it was meant to be. The other was a nightmare, and I have only now awakened.* (III.310)

While red represents passion, and white, emotionless purity, the combination suggests unity, especially in Christian symbolism. Weirwood trees are white with red leaves. Jon thinks that Ghost with his white fur and red eyes has similar coloring (V.466).

The Targaryen bastard Bloodraven is an albino, with white hair and skin is "pale as bone," who shoots with a white weirwood bow. His sigil is a single-headed white dragon with red eyes. His remaining eye is red, with a raven-shaped winestain birthmark. He wears "a cloak the color of smoke" ("The Mystery Knight," 734).

R'hllor is the god of fire and light; his devilish counterpart is a spirit of cold and darkness. The two may actually combine in harmony at series end.

Swords of ice and fire are the two blades forged from Ice into a Lannister red with the darkness of smoke. The Lannister-Stark conflict that could be said to have begun the war is fought between the icy gray and white bannered north and the red and gold bannered south. Proposed matches from Sansa and Joffrey to Sansa and Tyrion echo this conflict. Of course, the Stark children are born of Ice and Fire, with their redheaded mother from the warm south and their father, Warden of the North. Bran and Sansa resemble their mother, Arya and Jon, their father.

When Bran first sits on the Children of the Forest's weirwood throne, the sky above is described as dark, with red leaves and a pale sun (V.448). The throne itself is white weirwood and red branches (V.450). Several passages similarly combine the paleness of ice, red of leaves or blood, and darkness of dragonglass or the underground in a mystic combination of primal colors as characters explore Godswoods and ancient caves. The House of Black and White echoes this color scheme, as does the cave of the Brotherhood Without Banners under the Hill.

In an interview, Martin explained a bit about why his saga is called *Ice and Fire*, saying that the Wall and the dragons were "the obvious thing but yes, there's more." He noted:

> People say I was influenced by Robert Ford's poem [clearly, Robert Frost's poem is meant], and of course I was, I mean... Fire is love, fire is passion, fire is sexual ardor and all of these things. Ice is betrayal, ice is revenge, ice is... you know, that kind of cold inhumanity and all that stuff is being played out in the books. ("A Very Long Interview")

> Fire and Ice
> by Robert Frost, 1920

> Some say the world will end in fire,
> Some say in ice.
> From what I've tasted of desire

I hold with those who favor fire.
But if it had to perish twice,
I think I know enough of hate
To say that for destruction ice
Is also great
And would suffice.

Jojen's line to Bran, "If ice can burn, then love and hate can mate" sounds much like the poem (III.332). Maester Aemon adds, "Fire consumes, but cold preserves" (IV.383). The world may burn from the power of dragonfire, then freeze in the Long Winter. Both are terrible powers great enough to destroy the world. Martin comments, "I think the contrasts of ice and fire, of love and hate, all the things that they symbolize is one of the themes of what the series is about. You can't really encapsulate that in a nutshell, but that's certainly a part of it" (Shaw).

Weirwoods

The sun was sinking below the trees when they reached their destination, a small clearing in the deep of the wood where nine weirwoods grew in a rough circle. Jon drew in a breath, and he saw Sam Tarly staring. Even in the wolfswood, you never found more than two or three of the white trees growing together; a grove of nine was unheard of. The forest floor was carpeted with fallen leaves, bloodred on top, black rot beneath. The wide smooth trunks were bone pale, and nine faces stared inward. The dried sap that crusted in the eyes was red and hard as ruby. Bowen Marsh commanded them to leave their horses outside the circle. "This is a sacred place, we will not defile it."
When they entered the grove, Samwell Tarly turned slowly looking at each face in turn. No two were quite alike. "They're watching us," he whispered. "The old gods."
"Yes." Jon knelt, and Sam knelt beside him. (I.521-522)

There are many significant moments with weirwoods, the trees that dominate the old religion of the Starks and the First Men: Jaime has a dream of being torn between Brienne's path and Cersei's in the third book as he rests his head on a weirwood stump. Later, he treats honorably with a knight of the old ways, whose castle is dominated by a weirwood full of ravens. A thousand years past, "weird" meant destiny, so this is "destiny wood." "Were" actually means "man" in words like "werewolf," though with the Starks' wolf powers, this word root seems to relate as well. With pale bark and red sap, the trees bleed like human beings, emphasizing the great crime of cutting them down. The Eyrie cannot support a weirwood, and King's Landing has not planted one, showing how unfertile these places are for spiritual growth.

When, in the history of Westeros, Prince Daemon's wife tries to have his mistress killed, he retreats to Harrenhal to battle their enemies or die in the attempt. "Each night at dusk, he slashed the heart tree in the godswood to make the passing of another day. Thirteen marks can be seen upon that weirwood still, old wounds, deep and dark" that "bleed afresh every spring" ("The Princess and the Queen" 754). Thus his blood and pain is transferred to the tree.

The weirwoods are the focus of the Old Religion, a druid-like culture only still strong in the North. Once the children of the forest carved their faces and spoke through them, but their magic is mostly gone now.

> Brienne has her own weirwood encounter. "Most old castles had a godswood. By the look of it, the Whispers had little else. ... Mounds of poisonous red ivy grew over the heap of broken stones" (IV.416). There among the trees, Brienne battles rapists who call her "mad with

145

moon blood," a typical male insult for females (IV.420). She fights beside the sea and a dark cave, also feminine symbols of the primal, uncivilized world. Though the South has few remaining, Brienne sees a slender young weirwood tree "with a trunk as white as a cloistered maid" that echoes herself, just beginning to grow a feminine side in the midst of a masculine world (IV.416). (Frankel, *Women and Game of Thrones*, 143)

There among the old gods, she slays her enemies and wins the day.

The Brotherhood without Banners have a lair under a grove of weirwoods, with white roots all around. This represents a safe womb space, and also a place where Beric Dondarrion can be reborn each time. The Brotherhood take Arya to other weirwoods as they teach her:

> The next day they rode to a place called High Heart, a hill so lofty that from atop it Arya felt as though she could see half the world. Around its brow stood a ring of huge pale stumps, all that remained of a circle of once-mighty weirwoods. There were thirty-one, some so wide you could have use for a bed. High Heart had been sacred to the children of the forest, Tom Sevenstrings told her, and some of their magic lingered her still. No harm can ever come to those as sleep her, the singer said. It was said to be haunted by the ghosts of the children of the forest who had died here when the Andal king named Erreg the Kingslayer had cut down their grove. (III.301)

It's there that Arya meets a tiny woman who may be ghost or child of the forest and can see the present and future.

Weirwood is also used as a costly, pale decorative wood. The castle Whitewalls in "The Mystery Knight" is built with weirwood along with costly white stone from near the Eyrie. In the Eyrie itself, the throne of the Arryns is a seat carved of weirwood. In the Kingsguard White Tower, the wood appears as well:

> The table itself was old weirwood, pale as bone, carved in the shape of a huge shield supported by three white stallions. By tradition the Lord Commander sat at the top of the shield, and the brothers three to a side, on the rare occasions when all seven were assembled. (III.912)

It's unclear whether any of these were chosen for weirwood's magic or merely its expense and paleness. There are no faces here, but the wood still seems to have power. The Black Gate of the Nightfort still operates, with a face in the weirwood door, suggesting a lost power the other gates and furnishings may once have possessed. Likewise, weirwood bows are apparently the most powerful except for dragonbone.

Trees echo the sacred World Tree of Norse myth as well as the rituals of the Druids. Pliny wrote:

> The Druids - for so their magicians are called - held nothing more sacred than the mistletoe and the tree that bears it, always supposing that tree to be the oak. But they choose groves of oaks for the sake of the tree alone, and they never perform any of their rites except in the presence of a branch of it; so that it seems probable that the priests themselves may derive their name from the Greek word for that tree. In fact, they think that everything that grows on it has been sent from heaven and is a proof that the tree was chosen by the god himself.... (XVI)

Some heraldic devices from England bore an oak tree. "The reason lies in pre-Christian belief, in the old Celtic reverence for the oak, and its resulting association with kingship. Medieval sources record ruling families having at least one sacred tree outside the family's ring-fort" (Geoghegan). Thus the weirwoods are the ancient religion of the Druids, a path of blood and deeper wisdom for those who seek it. The trees and the Old Gods will play their part in the battle to come.

OTHER SYMBOLISM

Armor

Obviously knights wear armor, but some characters give it a different purpose. Brienne uses her massive, masculine armor for concealment until she doffs her helmet at Renly's tournament. In season four, Jaime gives Brienne a darker, more powerful suit of armor, acknowledging his respect for her as a strong knight.

Several ladies wear a corset-breastplate of a sort, suggesting a strength and combativeness over their demure silken gowns. Daenerys, presented with a sky blue silk gown in Qarth, wears a filigree gold corset over it to show her assertiveness. A hard gold breastplate featuring more lions was added to Cersei's red gown for her scenes during the Battle of the Blackwater. After Margaery begins wearing a sort of breastplate in King's Landing, Cersei does as well, responding to the younger woman's show of strength.

Poor Sansa has no physical defenses of any sort, even in her wardrobe. She insists "courtesy is a lady's armor," using a passive defensiveness in her speech as she has nothing else remaining. In the first episode, Tyrion says something similar to Jon Snow:

Tyrion Lannister: Let me tell you something, Bastard. Never forget what you are, the rest of the world will not. Wear it like armor and it can never be used to hurt you.
Jon Snow: What the hell do you know about being a bastard?
Tyrion Lannister: All dwarfs are bastards in their father's eyes.

Birth

Birth in the series is treated as unnatural and monstrous in a type of less-than-feminist body horror. Women should be alluring concubines, most often seen naked, but if they give birth, they become forces of destruction. Melisandre births her shadow creature in a chilling scene and sends it forth to do murder. Daenerys gives birth to a monster and nearly dies of it.

"He turned his face away. His eyes were haunted. "They say the child was ..." She waited, but Ser Jorah could not say it. His face grew dark with shame. He looked half a corpse himself.
"Monstrous," Mirri Maz Duur finished for him. The

> knight was a powerful man, yet Dany understood in that moment that the maegi was stronger, and crueler, and infinitely more dangerous. "Twisted. I drew him forth myself. He was scaled like a lizard, blind, with the stub of a tail and small leather wings like the wings of a bat. When I touched him, the flesh sloughed off the bone, and inside he was full of graveworms and the stink of corruption. He had been dead for years." (I.756)

In the prequel story "The Princess and the Queen," the princess has an equally monstrous birth:

> The princess shrieked curses all through her labor, calling down the wroth of the gods upon her half brothers and their mother the queen, and detailing the torments she would inflict upon them before she would let them die. She cursed the child inside her too. "Get out," she screamed, clawing at her swollen belly as her maester and her midwife tried to restrain her. "Monster, monster, get out, get out, GET OUT!" When the babe at last came forth, she proved indeed a monster: a stillborn girl, twisted and malformed, with a hole in her chest where her heart should have been and a stubby, scaled tail. (711)

Before the story begins, Lady Lannister dies having Tyrion, so his father hates him, and Elia of Dorne is killed because she has royal children. Lyanna may have died in childbirth. Lysa loses many babies and is inappropriate with her last son, whom she continues to breastfeed. Dalla dies giving birth. Gilly's is the only birth portrayed as positive and her child is to be given to the Others. Just after she has the child, her entire family is killed...at least, in the books.

Blood

"Bloody beef," "blood sausages," "blood melons," "blood oranges," red wine, and a nearly endless list of red juicy foods appear (pomegranates, blackberries, cherries, grapes, beets), all emphasizing the ongoing violence and war. Astapor is known for its red bricks, stained with the blood of its slaves. These people live in a violent world, in which they acknowledge even a birthing bed as a "women's battlefield." Cersei wears a dress with "a hundred dark red rubies" in the shape of teardrops to tell Sansa her father is a traitor (I.545). Jorah describes the Dothraki Sea for young Princess Daenerys, telling her that when it blooms it will be "all dark red flowers from horizon to horizon like a sea of blood" (I.226). Indeed, violence among the Dothraki blooms soon enough.

In the old days, Stark kings made blood sacrifices to heart trees (V.385). Maester Luwin may be evoking the same magic when he asks Osha to kill him and leave his body under the trees as Bran and Rickon escape. Underground, the Children give Bran a paste of weirwood seeds. Seeds represent untapped potential, and the natural cycle Bran is entering. It looks like blood to Bran, but he eats it nonetheless, accepting the assurance that "This will help awaken your gifts and wed you to the trees" (V.457).

Daenerys too learns that "Only blood can pay for blood." After losing Drogo and her unborn child, she lashes the Maegi to the funeral pyre and enters it herself, causing her dragons to be born.

> Following Mirri's equation of blood and sacrifice, Dany builds up Drogo's funeral pyre with his treasure, his body, the dragon eggs, and the bound Mirri Maz Duur, sentencing the woman to a fiery death. Then she, too, walks into the flames. By however such things are measured, the sacrifice is deemed a high enough price to pay to awaken the dragon eggs. (Scoble 132).

Melisandre has similar knowledge, but unlike Daenerys, she sacrifices those she cares nothing for, insisting on those with royal blood. Melisandre's magic may work, but she has not wrought such a dramatic miracle, or at least not yet. The Onion Knight tells Stannis, "I don't know if Robb Stark died because of the Red Woman's sorcery or because at war men die all the time, but I do know that uniting the Seven Kingdoms with blood magic is wrong. It is evil. And you are not an evil man" ("Mhysa"). There's an emphasis on royal blood, Targaryen blood, and so forth.

The dragons like those with Targaryen blood, and Targaryens presumably intermarried to continue the magic and dragon binding in their bloodline. Of course, in the Dance of the Dragons, new dragonriders are found on the streets –rumored but not proven to have Targaryen blood. Theon's uncle, Victarion Greyjoy, believes dragons can be controlled other ways. It's yet to be proven whether he's right.

Books

The bookish characters – Sam Tarly, Asha's Uncle Harlow, Prince Doran, Tyrion – all counsel prudence rather than charging into battle. While the series suggests the advice is wise, most hero characters refuse to take it.

Tyrion remarks, "My brother has a sword, and I have my mind. And a mind needs books like a sword needs a whetstone. That's why I read so much, Jon Snow" ("The Kingsroad"). Joffrey rejects his uncle Tyrion's wedding gift of a rare book and chops it to pieces, while Tyrion quietly remarks that Joffrey could have learned much about kingship from reading it.

Valiant, heedless Jaime may be learning wisdom, however. As he gazes at the White Book of the Kingsguard, he realizes his fate is his choice at last: "He could write what he chose henceforth" (III.1010). Shireen teaches Davos to read on the show, and he discovers the all-important letter from the Wall. Thus the ability to read changes the course of Westerosi future. This seems a foreshadowing of the hidden knowledge that must be found in time:

Old Nan's stories, told in the epic's beginning, actually seem to hold the key to defeating the Others...if only she'd been allowed to finish her tale. Castle Black has amazing records dating from before the Wall was raised, but many have faded until they're no longer legible, and only Sam seems prepared to read them. Oldtown appears to have impressive records as well, though the Maesters who study there have rejected magic. The children of the forest hold much old lore, though all is oral: "The singers of the forest had no books. No ink, no parchment, no written language...When they died, they went into the wood, into leaf and limb and root, and the trees remembered" (V.452). It appears the stories held by all these characters but mostly forgotten will be needed to save all of Westeros.

Candles

Candles are used in rituals the world over, as Jews light a candle to remember a deceased loved one, or Christians snuff then light a candle on Easter eve to symbolize Christ's death and resurrection.

> Candles play a great and varied role in churches, and according to their use and numbers the teaching of the Church is expressed symbolically. Examples of this are the six lights on the altar, representing the Church's constant round of prayer; the sanctuary lamp, Christ's Presence in the Tabernacle; the Eucharistic candles, symbolizing the coming of Christ in Communion; the Paschal candle, symbolical of the risen Christ during the Easter season. Candles are also symbolical when used in groupings: three candles represent the Trinity or seven candles signify the Seven Sacraments. (Ferguson)

In this manner, the people of Westeros light candles to one of the Seven in gratitude or humble prayer.

"As a symbol of the light of faith, the candle is an attribute of faith personified" (Shepherd 316). In their Citadel, the Maesters initiate their students by having them light a dragonglass candle. All fail, and the students of the fourth book explain this is meant to teach the limits of magic. One student explains:

> Even after he has said his vow and donned his chain and gone forth to serve, a maester will think back on the darkness of his vigil and remember how nothing that he did could make the candle burn...for even with knowledge, some things are not possible. (IV.9)

In fact, like the dragonglass daggers, this appears to be a tool of true magic that the maesters have forgotten.

> But this is not the lesson all take from the vigil. While most of the candles remain unlit, the acolytes holding them left brooding in the dark, there are others, like the one Leo Tyrell describes seeing in Marwyn's chambers in the Citadel, that burns with an unearthly flame. Slowly, despite the weight of history and the maesters' hope that magic is dead, the fantastic intrudes upon the mundane in ways that even the most logic-bound cannot deny.

(Scoble 128-129).

Magic has returned, even if the Maesters try to deny the very candles before them. As one Maester who clings to the old ways tells:

> All Valyrian sorcery was rooted in blood or fire. The sorcerers of the Freehold could see across mountains, seas, and deserts with one of these glass candles. They could enter a man's dreams and give him visions, and speak to one another half a world apart, seated before their candles. (IV.682)

This power may be needed to fight the darkness.

In the fifth book, Quaithe tells Daenerys "the glass candles are burning" (V.152-153). This indicates the return of magic along with the spells of the red priests and Daenerys's dragons. This may be more than a simple indicator: if the Others are vulnerable to obsidian, these candles may be a warning system to defend against them. The Maesters as a unit have not influenced the War of the Five Kings, or the upcoming war with the Others, but their stronghold keeps much hidden lore. As several main characters and their allies head in that direction, the truth may soon be revealed. Martin adds, "Oldtown *is* old, thousands of years old as opposed to King's Landing, which is only three hundred. Until Aegon's coming, it was the major city of Westeros. The Hightowers are one of the oldest families in the Seven Kingdoms" ("So Spake Martin" C91, P240). Perhaps they hold the missing knowledge our heroes need.

Chains

There are many chains in the series and many meanings behind them. Daenerys of course is the

156

"breaker of chains" in the east, freeing the slaves. Many slaves and prisoners are shown chained, and Daenerys emphasizes her role when she flings slave collars over the gates of Meereen, presenting the residents with a "choice." As she calls to them:

> I am not your enemy. Your enemy is beside you. Your enemy steals and murders your children. Your enemy has nothing for you but chains and suffering, and commands. I do not bring you commands. I bring you a choice. And I bring your enemies what they deserve. ("Breaker of Chains")

Terribly conflicted, Daenerys must later chain her dragons, compromising their freedom to avoid hurting her subjects. As such, she is a forger of chains as well as a breaker of them. A Meereenese wedding ceremony chains the bride and groom together, and Daenerys must accept that a marriage will threaten her freedom.

At the same time, maesters chain themselves to show they serve the realm, as servants to it not masters. As Jon puts it, "The collar is supposed to remind a maester of the realm he serves ... a chain needs all sorts of metals and a land needs all sorts of people" (I.450). Each maester forges a new link in a new metal for each subject he masters: Black iron (Ravenry), Bronze (Astronomy), Copper (History), Yellow Gold (Economics), Iron (Warcraft), Pale steel (Smithing), Silver (Medicine and healing), Valyrian steel (Magic and the occult).

Chains can symbolize interconnectivity or interdependence – all must work together or all perish. This is a meaning of the maester's chain of many metals and also the chain Tyrion makes for the Battle of Blackwater, which he sets every blacksmith in the city to forging. All must work together if the realm is to hold.

Chair Jostling

In "Walk of Punishment" there's a delightfully symbolic chair-jostling scene between Tywin, Littlefinger, Varys, Pycelle, Cersei, and Tyrion. Tywin, the new Hand, takes his seat and waits for the others. Varys, Littlefinger, and Pycelle hesitate, watching one another, until Varys (who has lasted longest in King's Landing) moves. Littlefinger desperately cuts him off and takes the closest chair to Tywin. Varys calmly takes the second, implying with his body language that he doesn't care, and Pycelle must take the third. Littlefinger-Varys-Pycelle end up sitting by Tywin in that order, like his trio of flunkies (which presumably they are).

Cersei moves her chair across from them, making a new place for herself that's just as good as theirs, rather than sit fourth in their trio. However, Tyrion one-ups that by *dragging* his chair, with a horrid squealing noise, across so he's at the foot of the table while Tywin is at the head. He's as far as possible from any of them, but still in a position of strength, gazing at his replacement. Tyrion is the one to break the silence and speak: "Intimate! *Lovely* table! Better chairs than the old small council chamber! Conveniently close to your own quarters, I like it!" His approval pits Tywin as his successor and equal, as Tyrion emphasizes that he will continue to mock and advise. In contrast with the Small Council of the first season (chairs all in a row, Ned Stark in the middle beside the empty chair of the king), this council is desperately jockeying for position.

Circles

"History is a wheel, for the nature of man is fundamentally unchanging," a scholar of the Iron Islands explains (IV.165). Certainly, the notion of history as a repeating cycle appears in the series. The heirs to the Targaryens, Starks, and Lannisters are dealing with the fallout of the Mad King and Robert's Rebellion against him. Robb fights his father's war but the Freys betray him in return for his betrayal. Daenerys wants to claim the crown of her father and brother. Prince Oberyn wants revenge for his sister Elia of Dorne, and King Robert wants to kill Daenerys for memory of her older brother, Crown Prince Rhaegar, who stole his beloved Lyanna. In turn,Cersei betrays him for still loving Lyanna, and the cycle continues.

> It all goes back and back, Tyrion thought, to our mothers and fathers and theirs before them. We are puppets dancing on the strings of those who came before us, and one day our own children will take up our strings and dance on in our steads. "Well, Prince Rhaegar married Elia of Dorne, not Cersei Lannister of Casterly Rock. So it would seem your mother won that tilt."
> "She thought so," Prince Oberyn agreed, "but your father is not a man to forget such slights. He taught that lesson to Lord and Lady Tarbeck once, and to the Reynes of Castamere. And at King's Landing, he taught it to my sister." (III.969)

There are too many characters to list who are named after fallen relatives, from Daenerys's dragons (named for her hero brother Crown Prince Rhaegar, coward brother Viserys, and husband Drogo) to Ned's children (named of course for Jon Arryn, Robert Targaryen, his older brother Brandon, and his father Rickon). Upon hearing her brothers are dead, Sansa dreams of having sons and giving them the same names. Talisa names her own child Ned, and he is as doomed as his namesake. There's a Rickard Karstark and Lyanna Mormont. There have been several Daenerys Targaryens, all with the power of prophecy.

Likewise, the gold hand of the king pin from the show grips the circle that surrounds it. The King's Hands, as Tyrion notes in season two, all seem to follow a similar pattern, acting honorably and being betrayed and killed for it. He attempts to break this pattern but is humiliated and demoted nonetheless.

Ser Barristan reflects that Daenerys's infatuation with Daario is weakening her throne, and compares it to all the doomed relationships of her family.

> Prince Rhaegar loved his Lady Lyanna, and thousands died for it. Daemon Blackfyre loved the first Daenerys, and rose in rebellion when denied her. Bittersteel and Bloodraven both loved Shiera Seastar, and the Seven Kingdoms bled. The Prince of Dragonflies loved Jenny of Oldstones so much he cast aside a crown, and Westeros paid the bride price in corpses.

He ends by noting that treason and turmoil followed forever after (V.875).

Cyvasse

Cyvasse is a Dornish game for two players. Each gets ten pieces with different powers and attributes: Rabble, Spearmen. Crossbowmen, Light Horse. Heavy Horse, Trebuchet, Catapult, Elephant, Dragon (the most powerful piece in the game), King. According to Martin, cyvasse was inspired by "a bit of chess, a bit of blitzkrieg, a bit of stratego. Mix well and add imagination" ("So Spake Martin" April 18, 2008).

Of course, chess can be compared to a game of thrones, with one king winning and the other losing. It's notable that chess or cyvasse is "a game of complete information," in which "all players are aware of each move up to the current point of the game" (Duval). The Game of Thrones is its antithesis in some ways, as secret moves, secret poisonings, secret agendas, and actions taken decades in the past all drive the characters of today.

Arianne of Dorne has much to learn about the game:

> "I told them to place a cyvasse table in your chambers," her father said when the two of them were alone.
> "Who was I supposed to play with?" Why is he talking about a game? Has the gout robbed him of his wits?
> "Yourself. Sometimes it is best to study a game before you attempt to play it. How well do you know the game, Arianne?"
> "Well enough to play."
> "But not to win. My brother loved the fight for its own sake, but I only play such games as I can win. Cyvasse is not for me" (IV.597-598)

In her strategies, which are too rash and discount many players, she reveals she's not yet ready for the Game. Nonetheless, she's sent forth again in book six, a mass of ambition without strong judgment.

> Arianne played a game of cyvasse with Ser Daemon, and another one with Garibald Shells, and somehow managed to lose both. Ser Garibald was kind enough to say that she played a gallant game, but Daemon mocked her. "You have other pieces beside the dragon, princess.

Try moving them sometime."
"I like the dragon."

Her heart is set, like Margaery's, on becoming *the* queen instead of allowing her duller brother to rule. For this she will need an alliance with dragons. When her father sends her on her mission, he hands her a black dragon from the cyvasse board.

Tyrion, who grows increasingly skilled, challenges Haldon the Halfmaester to a game, and Haldon says that the day Tyrion beats him is the day turtles swim out his arse. After the game, when someone asks when Haldon is, Tyrion replies, "He's taken to his bed, in some discomfort. There are turtles swimming out his arse" (V.189). Tyrion bets secrets as they play, linking the game with a real-world cunning. When he's finished he understands what game his companions are actually playing.

Tyrion also plays cyvasse as he tries to persuade Young Griff to change his strategies in the real world – Tyrion makes his point while beating the boy soundly.

> When the prince reached for his dragon, Tyrion cleared his throat. "I would not do that if I were you. It is a mistake to bring your dragon out too soon." He smiled innocently. "Your father knew the dangers of being over-bold." (V.279)
> …
> The dwarf pushed his black dragon across a range of mountains. "But what do I know? Your false father is a great lord, and I am just some twisted little monkey man. Still, I'd do things differently."
>   That got the boy's attention. "How differently?"
>   "If I were you? I would go west instead of east."
> (V.281)

Tyrion suggests Young Griff invade Westeros without Daenerys and her dragons. There's a wondrous story to appeal to a young man's pride of being a bold independent conqueror rather than a supplicant at the whims of a queen. However, Tyrion is likely giving bad advice:

> Smiling, he seized his dragon, flew it across the board. "I hope Your Grace will pardon me. Your king is trapped. Death in four."
> The prince stared at the playing board. "My dragon—"
> "—is too far away to save you. You should have moved her to the center of the battle."
> "But you said—"
> "I lied. Trust no one. And keep your dragon close."
> (V.282)

In their game, dragons are everything – the player with dragons wins. Tyrion's advice to "trust no one" also mimics Littlefinger's before he betrays Ned Stark. Tyrion later hears the boy took his advice and thinks of him as a bloody fool (V.366). It appears Tyrion has given the prince guidance that will destroy him. If he invades Westeros, he will be another army among many – only the invader with dragons stands a chance of winning militarily and gaining the people's support.

Meanwhile, Tyrion continues to play and beats the sellsword captain Ben Plumm repeatedly. In later games with the sellsword leader, he tries to tempt him to switch sides. As a scene from *The Winds of Winter* describes, "The white cyvasse dragon ended up at Tyrion's feet. He scooped it off the carpet and wiped it on his sleeve, but some of the Yunkish blood had collected in the fine grooves of the carving, so the pale wood seemed veined with red." Battle lies ahead. Also, as he has a white dragon piece and Arianne has a black one, they may be fighting on opposite sides as they back different dragons.

Credits

A close look at the credits reveals more than the setting for events of each episode: The sigils next to the actors' names correspond to their characters' Houses. Likewise, the astrolabe sun reveals the backstory as the stag, lion and direwolf unite to slay the dragon. The stag now wears a crown and the wolf and lion bow to it. This reflects the Stark-Tully-Lannister-Baratheon-Arryn alliance that brought down the Targaryens, though Tywin Lannister only joined when victory was inevitable.

Crossbows

Crossbows are something of an unskilled weapon, used at a distance. The first shot has an enormous punch, but as Yoren point out, there's a delay after. "I've always hated crossbows. Take too long to load!" he says, dying ("What is Dead may Never Die")

Attacked by peasants with crossbows in the Riverlands, Jaime turns snarky and easily defeats them:

> Crossbowman: Why are you on the run?
> Jaime: Killed some crossbowmen.

Tyrion uses a crossbow at the end of book three (and presumably season four) because he knows he's useless with a sword – a distance weapon is his only option.

Joffrey's favorite weapon is clearly the crossbow, a weapon that will keep him unharmed. In an early scene with Margaery, he explains the joy of hunting and killing things. He shows her what he describes as "Probably one of the finest weapons in the Seven Kingdoms," as he says. The weapons have a stunning amount of detail. Joffrey's crossbow perhaps more so than any. There's astounding gold filigree down every inch of its red surface. Lannister colors but also royal gold over bloody red. The quarrels are red and gold as well.

"I imagine it must be so exciting to squeeze your finger here and watch something die over there," she replies ("Dark Wings, Dark Words"). Natalie Dormer (Margaery) explains: "She is playing a role. She is trying to create a persona for herself that she thinks Joffrey will like and will trust and will listen to" (Vineyard).

She subtly seduces him not by touching him (a clear mistake as a pair of prostitutes once proved), but instead by touching his crossbow and fantasizing about how it must feel to hunt and kill. "The angle at which he holds his crossbow when firing will be immediately recognizable to anyone who sat through one of those 'subliminal sexual imagery in advertising' movies in school," Christopher Orr of *The Atlantic* notes ("Game of Thrones: A Feminist Episode"). As she (ahem) holds the tool of Joffrey's power, she's exerting control over him. Though he fights Cersei's attempt to boss him around earlier in the episode, he beams at Margaery's subtler approach. (Frankel, *Women and Game of Thrones* 104)

Natalie Dormer notes:

> You have to appreciate how badly that could have gone
> for her, too! Because Joffrey turned dark on a knife's
> edge the way he did with Sansa, and Margaery very
> quickly has to play a game of three-dimensional chess in
> her head to out-maneuver him and learn what makes him
> tick. That was the first scene I shot of the third series,
> Jack [Gleeson]'s and my first scene together. We didn't
> know each other as actors; we were trying to figure out
> the dynamic of how these two would interact, figure out
> each other's rhythms. But you have to marvel at
> Margaery – she passed the test, as it were. He's a very,
> very dangerous and tricky human being, and who knows
> what will happen in the future? Will she be so adept at
> out-maneuvering or fall foul of it the way Sansa
> did? (Vineyard)

In a truly chilling moment, he uses it to murder a helpless
bound Ros a few episodes later.

Dagger

A dagger can suggest treachery, as they are small
enough to be concealed in the clothing as Littlefinger
does when betraying Ned Stark. The all-important
dragonbone dagger used to attempt Bran's
assassination features heavily in the first season.
Many characters carry concealed weapons that prove
deadly at close quarters. Cersei thinks, "This was how
an enemy should be dealt with: with a dagger, not a
declaration (IV.249-250). Melisandre foresees
"daggers in the dark" surrounding Jon in the fifth book
(V.59).

Blades reflect the heroes who wield them: Sam
slays a wight with a dragonglass dagger, quickly
becoming a hero of the Night's Watch. Mirri Maz Duur
has a particular sacrificial knife. "It looked old;

hammered red bronze, leaf-shaped, its blade covered
with ancient glyphs" (I.711). Daario has his suggestive
blades with naked women for hilts. As he caresses
them, Daenerys imagines him caressing her. His show
blades are even more suggestive, with the blade
protruding from between the woman's legs.

Dragon Eggs

> Viserys: If I sell one egg, I'll have enough to buy a ship.
> Two eggs, a ship and an army.
> Jorah: And you have all three.
> Viserys: I need a large army. ("A Golden Crown")

Viserys sees only wealth, while Daenerys
understands how to awaken the ancient magic.

> "Bring me ... egg ... dragon's egg ... please ..." ... When
> she woke the third time, a shaft of golden sunlight was
> pouring through the smoke hole of the tent, and her arms
> were wrapped around a dragon's egg. It was the pale
> one, its scales the color of butter cream, veined with
> whorls of gold and bronze, and Dany could feel the heat
> of it. Beneath her bedsilks, a fine sheen of perspiration
> covered her bare skin. Dragondew, she thought. Her
> fingers trailed lightly across the surface of the shell,
> tracing the wisps of gold, and deep in the stone she felt
> something twist and stretch in response. It did not
> frighten her. All her fear was gone, burned away. (I.754-
> 755)

Daenerys is seen communing with the eggs one-
on-one through the first book and season, as if they
are meant for her. "Daenerys's perception of warmth
in her dragon eggs is not available to others. She feels
them as warm, nearly hot, and comes to believe that
they are ready to hatch if they can be placed in a hot

enough fire; but Ser Jorah Mormont attests that the eggs feel cool to the touch" (Cox 136).

"Dany never flinches from heat, and she dreams of dragons taking wing and breathing fire. When her patron, Illyrio Mopatis, gives her three petrified dragon eggs as a wedding gift, we can be certain something will hatch from them, either figuratively or literally" (Scoble 130). As Daenerys holds the eggs, tends them, heats them in the brazier, she is metaphorically tending herself, encouraging herself to grow. They travel on each step of the journey with her, and she confides her hopes and fears to them, trying to hatch them as her own pregnancy swells. When she hatches them in the fire, she hatches herself, turning from princess to queen.

> She has become a worker of miracles, mother to the first dragons in centuries. When Dany sees her subjects kneel, she knows they're hers as they were never Drogo's—won by the power of life and fire, not that of conquering and rule. On the threshold of death, she calls herself Daenerys Stormborn of House Targaryen for the first time. She's claiming her own birthright of dragons and the Targaryen legacy, not just her role as Drogo's counterpart. "All her fear was gone, burned away" (I.755). (Frankel, Women and *Game of Thrones* 153)

Eggs symbolize potential, as seeds do. They are birth and life and rebirth, so they are eaten at the spring festivals of Easter and Passover, and often consumed after funerals.

> Because eggs embody the essence of life, people from ancient times to the modern day have surrounded them with magical beliefs, endowing them with the power not only to create life but to prophesy the future. Eggs symbolize birth and are believed to ensure fertility. They

> also symbolize rebirth, and thus long life and even immortality. Eggs represent life in its various stages of development, encompassing the mystery and magic of creation. Creation myths commonly describe how the universe was hatched from an egg, often laid by some mythical water bird swimming in the primordial waters... (Andrews 86)

As such, they're a logical gift for Daenerys at her wedding as she embarks on a new journey of transformation. The *Game of Thrones* producers gave George R.R. Martin one of Daenerys's dragon eggs as a wedding gift when he married Parris McBride in February 2011.

Egg from the Dunk and Egg stories has a similar plot arc.

> His nickname, in fact, has at least three meanings: of course, "Egg" is a shortened form of "Aegon"; it is an appropriate name for a bald boy, as Dunk notes—"His head does look like an egg"; and the egg is regularly employed as a symbol of rebirth. In a sense, Egg is being reborn, as he sheds the clothing and duties of a prince to begin learning about life from the new perspective of a common man. Indeed, when Dunk first sees Egg, he is stark naked, emerging from a bath in a stream, much like a newborn child. (Westfahl 62)

His brother Aemon (one day to be Maester Aemon of the Wall) tells him Westeros needs an Aegon to rule, not an egg, so he must kill the boy within himself and allow the man to be born. In the short story "The Mystery Knight," visions of a dragon hatching are realized in Egg, who grows from child to leader. Brynden Rivers, the king's spymaster, explains, "Daemon dreamed that a dragon would be born at Whitewall and it was. The fool just got the color wrong" (735).

Dragonglass

The rangers once knew dragonglass could defend them, so they buried a stockpile at the Fist of the First Men. The Children of the Forest used to give the Night's Watch a hundred dragonglass daggers each year (V.100). On the show and in the books, Sam makes it clear that dragonglass in the same as obsidian.

On earth this is volcanic glass, created by the molten heat of the earth. Obsidian is most notable for its sheen, though it also creates a very sharp edge. It was used for divination mirrors and astronomically linked with Saturn, god of chaos and change. Mirrors are seen as bringing truth. They could also frighten off spirits and banish demons.

To the Westerosi, obsidian is a token of the Stone Age and lost knowledge of the past. It was the tool of the Children of the Wood. As it comes from Dragonstone Isle or the Children of the Wood, it's unclear whether this is in fact made occasionally (or exclusively) by dragons. Martin hints at an answer:

> Martin: Obsidian is of course volcanic glass; it's formed by immense heat and pressure down in the earth. The dragons themselves are creatures of intense heat.
> Shaw: I wasn't sure if you had added something to obsidian for the fantasy.
> Martin: I've given it magical characteristics that of course real obsidian doesn't necessarily have. After all, we live in a world that has no magic. My world does have magic, so it's a little bit different. (Shaw)

Tyrion examines the Targaryen dragon skulls and sees each is "black as onyx due to its high iron content." The teeth are "long, curving knives of black diamond" (I:121). Daenerys's three eggs too "shimmered like polished metal" and are heavy as stone (I:104). Are dragon bones and dragon eggs the source of dragonglass? Or merely similar?

The Doom of Valyria, a great explosion of a volcano chain, may be related to dragons as well. A century before the homeland of dragons and magic exploded, the Targaryens set forth, but stopped at Dragonstone, until after the Doom. Daenerys the Dreamer saw they should leave, but it's unclear why Dragonstone, not Westeros, was their goal. Perhaps the single island had the volcanoes or dragonglass they needed to breed their dragons. "Odd, that," Tyrion thinks. "Dragonstone is no more than a rock. The wealth was farther west, but they had dragons. Surely they knew that it was there" (V.76). Was there another reason Dragonstone was essential for them? Dragonstone, with its sculptures and gargoyles throughout, appears to hold more than only the stone. There are rumors of dragon eggs, though they must be well hidden for Stannis not to find and sell them. Martin comments, "If you look at how the citadel of Dragonstone was built and how in some of its structures the stone was shaped in some fashion with magic... yes, it's safe to say that there's something of Valyrian magic still present." ("Interview in Barcelona")

Game of Thrones

Martin adores strategy games –he played so much *Call of Cthulu* and *Superworld* in a year that he stopped writing and nearly went bankrupt (Vizzini 204). As such, there's a strong echo of gaming in the series and its structure. Several popular games have spun off the series –board, card, and computer. At his strategy board, Robb moves symbols that resemble game pieces, emphasizing that he's playing a literal game. Stannis too looms over the Painted Table of Aegon the Conqueror, covered with pieces for the armies.

> [Gaming] informs the title of the first volume in the series and manifests in the works themselves in interesting ways, from the thematic treatment of games—the things the characters view as games, or, more often, mistake as nothing more than diversions, is a variation of the confounded expectations game—to the story's basic structure, with the tightly focused individual chapters functioning quite like the movement of discrete units in a miniatures battle (Lowder xv-xvi)

Of course, the "game of thrones" itself refers to a game of alliances, threats, lies, secrets, and much more, until one gains power. Famously, Cersei tells Ned in the first season, "When you play the Game of Thrones, you win or you die. There is no middle ground" ("You Win or You Die"). In next scene, she's killed the king and moves against Ned as well. Certainly, many characters keep their agendas a secret – some want to place another on the throne, or rule behind the scenes. As R. Shannon Duval explains in an essay on game theory in the series:

> If it is true that when playing the game of thrones Lannister-style, "you win or you die," then all players have an important stake in the game. It is also safe to assume that players are ultimately concerned with their expected payoffs, although discovering a player's true endgame is often half of the game itself. (252)

If Margaery wants to be "the" queen, Stannis is in her way, but is Cersei? Joffrey and Tommen? Varys says he serves the realm, but he appears to prefer his own candidate to peace. Does Dorne only want revenge, or do its players crave power as well?

There are also players who play badly through irrationality, and players like Cersei playing to see her children succeed, though for the most part the players are family and strategic alliances (the Lannisters play mainly as a team with the Tyrells mainly supporting them) contrasted with characters like Jon Snow or Arya who remove themselves from play.

Players constrained by honor and truth generally play worst. Jaime Lannister quips, "Give me an honorable opponent and I will sleep better at night" (I.82). Ned Stark, with his blunt questions and direct threats, fares as badly as Jon Arryn does, for the same reason. Stannis loses on the Blackwater as his straightforward assault falls to dishonorable wildfire and a masquerade of Renly's ghost. His murderous shadows, however, destroy one of the five kings. "An honorable enemy does not lie, cheat, steal, or poison. An honorable enemy will not break an oath or turn his cloak" (Duval 252).

Of course, many characters must fight with only the tools of their physical skills and modest holdings. Describing the honorable duel he fought for Catelyn as a youth, Littlefinger notes, "Do you know what I learned, losing that duel? I learned that I'll never win, not that way. That's their game, their rules" ("You Win or You Die").

He, Varys, and (to a lesser extent) Pycelle prioritize playing above all – they aren't lords or kings or lovers or fathers – they only exist in King's Landing to manipulate others and be the power behind the throne. Littlefinger says, "In King's Landing, there are two sorts of people. The players and the pieces" (III.933). He notes that Sansa has been only a piece for the Lannisters and Tyrells to marry for her lands, but she can learn to be a player if she wishes. Thus far her subtle manipulations have been to save lives or put them in danger, but not to gain worldly power for herself.

By contrast, Tyrion grows in influence, particularly in season two. Varys tells Tyrion, "You're quite good at being Hand, you know. Jon Arryn and Ned Stark were good men, honorable men. But they disdained the game and those who play it. You enjoy the game. And you play it well" ("The Prince of Winterfell"). He's a clever observer of human nature and unusually aware of his position, without the illusions that blind Ned. Tyrion manipulates Lysa Arryn to grant him a trial by combat or be seen to break the law, and leverages himself a dishonorable sellsword who will fight for coin and win. He manipulates the hill tribes as well, in both cases making himself more valuable if he's safe and alive. Later, he understands Shae is his weakness and keeps many layers of secrecy and protection around her.

Varys' choices are intriguing as he and Illyrio play a game over decades. He may actually confess part of the truth to Tyrion on the show:

> Tyrion: What do you want? Tell me.
> Varys: If we're going to play, you'll have to start.

Tyrion describes how much he's enjoyed being Hand. After they've discussed the gods, Varys pauses, indicating a topic shift. He then says with surprising intensity, "This morning, I heard a song all the way from Qarth, beyond the red wastes. Daenerys Targaryen lives" ("The Prince of Winterfell").

As he shows by book five, Varys and Illyrio want a Targaryen heir on the throne (or at least someone who appears Targaryen and may at least in part share in the bloodline). Illyrio notes: "There is no peace in Westeros, no justice, no faith...and soon enough, no food. When men are starving and sick of fear, they look for a savior...A savior comes from across the sea to bind up the wounds of Westeros" (V.30).

Illyrio's worship of the Lord of Light may be a motivation, or either or both schemers may be related to the exiled Targaryen bastards known as the Blackfyres or their chosen candidate. Varys and Illyrio scheme in book one to make a Stark-Lannister civil war...though not until the time is right. They don't want everyone uniting under one king to battle Daenerys's Dothraki – they want fragmented alliances and paranoia in the face of a possible Dothraki invasion. Varys thus convinces Ned to make peace with the Lannisters and delay the civil war...until irrational Joffrey executes him. Civil war begins, sooner than the conspirators planned. Then Daenerys miraculously awakens the three dragon eggs Illyrio gave her – something unprecedented in all of history. There's a new player and a new game.

Gates

Several important gates feature in the series. The Freys have twin towers with strong gates that Robb must negotiate to pass. The Wall has a fierce battle fought at its gates between Donal Nye the blacksmith and a giant. It also has gates of magic, where Sam lets Bran and his friends cross (in the books) by persuading a weirwood face that he's of the Night's Watch, the gate's sworn defender.

The Eyrie has its infamous Bloody Gate, with the Blackfish as Gatekeeper. As Lysa shuts her gates and won't allow Robb's army to pass through her territory, she guards them as she does her chastity, and they come to symbolize it. The Virgin Mary is sometimes referred to as the Closed Gate, in reference to her unblemished virginity. She is also given the tile "Gate of Heaven" because she is the Mediatrix of All Graces.

In Christian art, the gate signifies death and departure from life in this world. "...Thou hast liftest me up from the gates of death" (Psalm 9:15). As such, all these gates start to echo the great gate of life and death, perhaps the same as the "curtain" that the Other waits behind or the "curtain" Melisandre sees Jon Snow crossing in her visions.

Hair

Hairstyles are elaborate in court and simple elsewhere: Catelyn and Talisa wear their hair practically as they're on battlefields, while Margery and Cersei have their hair done in intricate loops and plaits. Sansa's hair indicates her allegiance, as she mimics Cersei's style in the first season and Margaery's in the third. Tyrion cuts off Grand Maester Pycelle's beard in the second book, and he looks far less dignified after. When Tyrion frees him, he comments, "I could swear that I hadn't harmed a hair on his head, but it wouldn't be strictly true" (II.448).

The men of Meereen have significant hairstyles in the book:

> Ghiscari hair was dense and wiry; it had long been the fashion for the men of the Slaver Cities to tease it into horns and spikes and wings. By shaving, Skahaz had put old Meereen behind him to accept the new. His Kandaq kin had done the same after his example. Others followed, though whether from fear, fashion, or ambition, Dany could not say; shavepates, they were called. Skahaz was the Shavepate... and the vilest of traitors to the Sons of the Harpy and their ilk. (V.37)

The moderate Hizdahr keeps his hair midlength in a sort of compromise as he tries to bridge the gap between Daenerys and Old Ghis.

Hair color is significant in books and show as an issue of lineage – the Lannisters have golden hair and the Baratheons have black, no matter the mother's hair color (biologically speaking this is inaccurate – on earth at least – but in Westeros it forms a significant plot point). The "true" Targaryens have hair of silver-gold (white on the show) and purple eyes, while Targaryens with less of the magic in them may have other coloring.

In the books, Robb, Sansa, Bran, and Rickon have Tully red hair like their mother, which emphasizes their blend of ice and fire – southern mother and northern father. The Red Priestess has red hair as Thoros of Myr does, but her red eyes suggest magic or artificiality rather than a natural color.

Hand

Hands and hand symbolism are vital to the saga. There's the position of Hand of the King, the man who does the king's dirty work and aids him. Ned (season one) Tyrion (season two) and Tywin (seasons three and four) all bring different methods to the role, as Jon Arryn once did. In the books, the Hand wears a gold chain of linked hands, while on the show, it's a simpler pin.

The militant arm of the Lord of Light in Volantis is called the Fiery Hand. The metaphor appears similar to the King's Hand – the active branch of the faith. It's unclear what role they'll play in books six and seven, but they may potentially be an army of Melisandres.

Jaime loses his right hand early in season three.

This is a castration for him, as he can no longer fight, write, or even cut his own meat. Nonetheless, his ordeal seems to bring him a greater understanding of honor. Heroes lose a hand in many tales from *Lord of the Rings* (Beren One-Hand from the Silmarillion) to Celtic myth. A severed hand is also seen in heraldry:

The severed red right hand (dexter hand couped at the wrist gules) is a feature of many coats of arms for families of the Uí Neill (i.e. descendants of Niall). This same symbol is associated with the province of Ulster and appears on the Arms of that province and on the modern flag of Northern Ireland. There are at least three explanations of its origins. The first relates to the name of the son of Bolg or Nuadu, the Sun God of the Celts, and by some accounts the divine progenitor of all Celts. This son was known as Labraid Lámhdhearg (Labraid of the Red Hand). The association of the symbolic red hand with the Sun God, therefore makes it an appropriate heraldic icon.

The second relates to Nuada, king of the Tuatha Dé Danann, who had his right hand severed by Sreng during a great battle with the Fomorians. No imperfect man being allowed to hold the throne, Nuada was forced to abdicate in favour of Bres. However, a silver hand was fashioned for him and the power of ancient magic was used to cause flesh and sinew to grow back around the prosthesis. When Bres died, Nuada again assumed his royal place. The third explanation is somewhat more fanciful. The story tells of a pact among the seven sons of Miledh of Esbain, the Celtic king who sons conquered Ireland that the ruler of the new land would be whosoever among them first touched the soil of the island. As the flotilla approached the shore, one of the sons took his sword, cut off his right hand and threw it to land, thus becoming the ruler. (Geoghegan)

Cersei commissions a beautiful golden hand for Jaime on season four of the show, covered in delicate filigree swirls that suggest her influence twining over him. In the book, he orders it made, and it's likely simpler.

There are an enormous number of other hand injuries in the story: Jon Snow burns his hand battling the wight. In the books, the wright's hand is in turn brought to King's Landing as proof. Coldhands is named for a particular attribute. Davos and Qhorin Halfhand have lost fingers, as Theon has. Theon also loses a young uncle to the "finger game" (played with axes) when his wound turns bad. Victarion Greyjoy and Jon Connington have severe hand injuries in the fifth book. Another set of hands appear with the murdered slave children, whose hands point the way to Meereen. Daenerys takes a fearful vengeance on the men who thus slaughter innocents.

Littlefinger comes from the smallest of the "fingers," five peninsulas not far from the Eyrie. Their grasping appearance on maps resembles Littlefinger's own grasp for power. By contrast, Davos considers his fingerbones to be his luck, and many tines remarks that he lost his luck (literally the bones) on the Blackwater. "He had been a better man and a braver one with that bag of bones around his neck" (III.862).

In fact, four of his sons die in the battle in the books (one on the show). Stannis loses faith in him and consigns him to the cells. Both characters must climb to power, finger by finger, as they manipulate kings and discover new roads from their humble origins to winning the game.

Hexagon

The mysterious Quaithe wears a mask of hexagons, echoing the setting of Melisandre's ruby pendent. Costume designer Michele Clapton wanted to tie the two characters together since they both hail from shadowy Asshai. The hexagram, or six pointed star, was an ancient symbol for the union of male and female. The hexagon has similar associations as a six-pointed symbol of balance, equality and integration. Islamic art uses many hexagons, symbolizing the six directions (Shepherd 335). Both Melisandre and Quaithe work magic, using their power to control motion and direction and also watch the world as it changes around them. They may be bringing about a union of male and female, as Melisandre councils heroes of ice, Stannis and Jon, while Quaithe counsels the heroine of fire.

Horn

"Sharp as a swordthrust, the sound of a horn split the air. Bright and baneful was its voice, a shivering hot scream that made a man's bones seem to thrum within him. The cry lingered in the damp sea air: aaaaRREEEEeeeeeeeeeeeeeeee" (IV.227).

In Old Valyria, Theon's uncle discovers a mysterious horn of fire called Dragonbinder that's fabled to control dragons. Black with red gold and Valyrian steel, it burns the lungs of those who blow it. Its inscription of "Blood for Fire, Fire for Blood" matches the Targaryen motto, "Fire and Blood" and also the concept that life must pay for magic. "The horn must be claimed with blood—only death may pay for life, or power, as it were" (Scoble 137). In fact, the man who blows it dies. By book six, Victarion Greyjoy is approaching Meereen, where dragons still remain. Will he control one successfully or will he perish in the attempt?

There are other significant horns in the series. Claw Isle has "a horn that could summon monsters from the deep" (III.493). Krakens perhaps? Are there such things as sea dragons? Mermaids? The Wildlings find an ancient horn, long and black with bands of old gold (III.1018). Last and terribly powerful is the fabled Horn of Joramun, or Horn of Winter, said to be able to bring down the Wall or awaken "giants from the earth" (II.376). The horn that can bring down the mightiest of walls must be compared to the horns at Jericho which did just that in the Bible. If it's the horn Sam and Jon find with the obsidian weapons on the Fist of the First Men, it was treasured by Rangers (who could have shattered it to protect the Wall instead of keeping it close). Does it have some other use then? Can it summon and control an Ice Dragon, like the one rumored to dwell under the Wall? Could it bring down other walls like the "curtain of light at the end of the world?" (I.136-137)

Jung saw the horn as a spear and container in one – a melding of masculine and feminine (Cirlot 151). It offers the magic of the cornucopia, the strength of the bull, and the prosperity of the drinking cup. Horns of ice and fire bring a similar balance, like that between male and female symbolism. It's likely the power of both will be needed to win the day.

A final horn is the one the Night's Watch blows for warning: one for rangers returning, two for Wildlings attacking, a fabled three for Others attacking. In their oath, they call themselves "the horn that wakes the sleepers." With a horn of fire and one of ice, they may find themselves the Watch's greatest weapon. Celts used horns to make a great clamor in battle and frighten off the enemy. "As a musical instrument, it figures in emblems symbolizing the spiritual call to join the holy war" (Cirlot 151). The horn is the Egyptian hieroglyph for elevation and glory as it allows its wielder to open a path. With all these symbols combined, horns may prove as mighty as swords.

Iron and Bronze

Robb has an iron and bronze crown, the way the warrior kings of the North made them. As such, he proclaims himself a fighter rather than a soft king of gardens and gold. Aegon the Conqueror wore an "iron-and-ruby crown" suggesting conquest and blood ("Princess and the Queen" 711). Iron and bronze are metals of war – cold, solid, and purposeful. Stannis insists, "Laws should be made of iron, not pudding" (V.54).

Similarly, Jaqen gives Arya an iron coin with the Faceless Man on it, so she can become an assassin if she wishes. At the end of season three, Arya offers her iron coin to a Frey soldier, and as he bends down to pick it up, she pulls out a dagger and repeatedly stabs him. A similar coin appears when Daario draws it and is chosen to kill Daenerys on the show. The coin represents death: black, cold, and all-too-real.

The Iron Islands with their Ironborn men and "Iron" ship names likewise emphasize the stark coldness and warlike nature of their men. Balon Greyjoy announces: "No man gives me a crown. I pay the iron price. I will take my crown. That is who I am. That is who we have always been" ("The Night Lands"). However, the books note, "Robert was the true steel. Stannis is pure iron, black and hard and strong, yes, but brittle, the way iron gets. He'll break before he bends (III.1055). Balon Greyjoy is too hard, too proud, too unwilling to compromise.

Bronze is the military material of the past – the First Men wielded bronze swords and large leather shields:

> When men arrived, they burned the woods and protective faces. The children fought, and the greenseers made the waters rise, smashing the Broken Arm of Dorne that had enabled men to cross. But the men, armed with bronze, were winning. At last, men and children signed the Pact: men would live in the coastlands and meadows, the children now they live only in dreams would take the deep woods…The Andals brought the new gods and conquered all but the north. (I.736-37)

The Crannogmen, in their footsteps, fight with bronze knives and frog spears. The Unsullied wear spiked bronze caps. There are many bronze statues, from the horses at Vaes Dothrak to Theon's promise to make a bronze statue to his men when he fights at Winterfell. Several halls have bronze gates. The Reeds also swear by bronze and iron in their oath:

"To Winterfell we pledge the faith of Greywater.
Hearth and harvest and we yield up to you, my lord. Our
swords and spears and arrows are yours to command.
Grant mercy to our weak, help to our helpless, and
justice to all, and we shall never fail you."
"I swear it by earth and water" (the old ways, nature,
the old gods of the Heart Trees)
"I swear it by bronze and iron" (the old ways, the
arms of man and also the ancient Stark crown)
"We swear it by ice and fire" (the ancient war and the
ancient magics) (II.329) .

Bran has never learned these words, either because they're
so old they've passed out of fashion or because the Reeds
made them for this occasion. Either way, their father
communed with the children of the wood at the Isle of
Faces and Jojen is a greenseer. Whether this is from the
pact of the First Men or a premonition of forces at play, the
Reeds know where to place their faith.

Iron Throne

Cersei: You should have taken the realm for yourself.
Jaime told me about the day King's Landing fell.
He was sitting in the Iron Throne and you made him give
it up. All you needed to do was climb the steps yourself.
Such a sad mistake.
Ned: I've made many mistakes in my life, but that wasn't
one of them. ("You Win or You Die")

The Iron Throne is made of the melted spears of
Aegon the Conqueror's enemies, as he took their
seven kingdoms one by one. Littlefinger says that
while the Iron Throne is rumored to have over 1000
swords, it really only has about 200 – he counted
("The Climb"). The throne may be only an exaggerated
symbol of power but it's a necessary one. Cersei
reflects in book four that she cannot take young king
Tommen to Casterly Rock, because he must be seen to

rule from King's Landing, the seat of power since Aegon the Conqueror. Martin notes that the throne on the show is smaller and more elegant than he intended it.

> The main difference is scale. The Iron Throne that's described in the books is gigantic. It's huge. There's actually a scene in the show where Littlefinger talks about the thousand swords of Aegon's enemies, and says, "Well, there's not really a thousand swords. That's just a tale we tell ourselves." And David and Dan made a brilliant speech of that, because there clearly are not a thousand swords in that one. But in the real one, the one in the books, there really are a thousand swords! Maybe two thousand swords! You have to climb a steep set of steps, and it's ugly, and it's asymmetric. This one, it looks dangerous, with the spikes, but it has a certain beauty and a symmetry to it. The throne in the books, there's a point made that it was hammered together by blacksmiths, not by furniture designers. It was meant to be a symbol of conquest and triumph, and, you know: "Look. I took the swords form these people and hammered them in. Now I park my ass on top of them." It has a message there. (*Vanity Fair*)

Littlefinger comments, "Do you know what the realm is? It's the thousand blades of Aegon's enemies, a story we agree to tell each other over and over until we forget that it's a lie" ("The Climb"). In "The Climb," Varys and Littlefinger call the Iron Throne an "ugly old thing" yet agree it has a certain attraction. Varys then calls it "The Lysa Arryn of chairs" as Littlefinger leaves to woo her.

Many rulers are unfit to sit on the throne, so it cuts them, as the legends go. When Mad King Aerys was only forty years old, he looked ancient and haggard. He cut his hands and thighs so many times on the Iron

Throne that some called him "King Scab" behind his back (IV.232).

The queen from the Dance of the Dragons fares just as badly at her coronation. "Although Rhaenyra was in armor, those present witnessed the throne leaving several cuts on her legs and left hand. The dripping blood was taken as a sign that the throne had rejected her; her days as ruler would be few (741). At the end of *A Clash of Kings*, while the victors are rewarded and punished, Joffrey cuts himself on the Iron Throne and runs crying out of the throne room. King Robert tells Ned, "It *is* a monstrous uncomfortable chair. In more ways than one" (I.117).

Magic

In the House of the Undying, Pyat Pree explains that the dragons have returned and brought magic back to the world. "It is strongest in their presence," he says, "and they are strongest in yours" ("Valar Morghulis"). With the rebirth of her dragons, the White Walkers have also returned. It's unclear which event is effect and which cause, or whether a larger cause is pushing both.

Daenerys herself has a great deal of magic in her: "It is said that the Targaryens have features that reflect their links to the magical, what they refer to as 'blood of the dragon.' Dany never flinches from heat, and she dreams of dragons taking wing and breathing fire" (Scoble 130). While the Targaryen powers of prophecy and dragon riding are well-known, they're also subtle. Martin comments:

> The proper use of magic is one of the trickiest aspects of writing fantasy. If badly done, it can easily unbalance a

book....Middle Earth is a world full of wonders, beyond a doubt, but very little magic is actually performed on stage. Gandalf is a wizard, for instance, but he does most of his fighting with a sword. That seemed to be a much more effective way to go than by having someone mumbling spells every paragraph, so I tried to adapt a similar approach in *A Game of Thrones*. ("So Spake Martin" C90, P120)

As Edward Cox adds in his essay, "Magic, Knowledge, and Metaphysics in *A Game of Thrones*," "The elusive nature of these magical events [prophetic dreams proven true] raises the question of whether supernatural events could occur in our world" (Cox 137). Subtle means possible, in a way flashy magic does not.

As the dragons and White Walkers reappear in the world, other types of magic come as well. Thoros of Myr (traveling with the Brotherhood without Banners in season three) says in "The Climb":

It's a terrible thing to say, but by the time I came to Westeros, I didn't believe in our Lord. I decided that He, that all the gods, were stories we told the children to make them behave. So I wore the robes and every now and then I'd recite the prayers, but it was just for show. A spectacle for the locals. Until the Mountain drove a lance through this one's heart. I knelt beside his cold body and said the old words. Not because I believed in them, but...he was my friend and he was dead. And they were the only words I knew. And for the first time in my life, the Lord replied. Beric's eyes opened and I knew the truth. Our god is the one true god. And all men must serve Him.

It's notable that the previous times he said the words, nothing happened. His powers only awakened after Daenerys's dragons were born. Since Melisandre is first seen in *A Clash of Kings* and the beginning of season two, her powers may be just as new. The Maegi of R'hllor appear to know much about the Other and the battle of ice and fire to come, but it's uncertain whether they've had power before recently.

The Maesters, however, view magic with less delight. They view the dragonglass candles as an exercise in futility, though once they worked. They appear to have eradicated magic from the world in the past and even slain the dragons. "The world the Citadel is building has no place in it for sorcery or prophecy or glass candles, much less for dragons" they insist (IV.683).

> Given the aura of unreliability surrounding the subject, it should not be a surprise, then, to learn that the maesters, who are some of the most educated and learned characters in Westeros, have a conflicted relationship with magic. They acknowledge it existed at one time, but few look upon it favorably. Not many study magic enough to gain a Valyrian steel link in their chain, and those who do are often regarded as strange. Still others, like House Stark's Maester Luwin, seem almost jaded and bitter to find no substance in magic. (Scoble 127-128).

Needle

Jon tells Arya before they part, "You'll be sewing all through winter. When the spring thaw comes, they will find your body with a needle still locked tight between your frozen fingers" (I.75). Arya hates needlework, but she finds an alternative, blending the feminine symbol with her thin, light sword, naming it as a woman's weapon, not a man's.

Master Syrio tells her she must fight delicately, carefully. She learns to fight, swift and sudden as a needle. When she loses the sword for a time, she finds herself captured and drifting from captivity to captivity: Tywin Lannister, the Brotherhood Without Banners, the Hound. She also loses her direction after her family's death. Though she bides her time, she's eager to reacquire her identity.

"'Course you named your sword" the Hound smirks in "Two Swords." When she sees Polliver with Needle, Arya bides her time and then takes it. Her proud smile on the show with new sword and new horse makes all clear. Maisie Williams (Arya) adds: "In this moment after she's killed Polliver, she's realized her own power as well. ... She's definitely kind of changing and putting on a more brutal approach to things. It's a lot more risky, as well, but she's not afraid of death" (Hibberd, "Maisie Williams"). From her first unplanned killings, Arya is getting more and more brutal.

In the fourth book, she must give up her identity, but Needle she keeps, because "Needle was Robb and Bran and Rickon, her mother and her father, even Sansa Needle was Winterfell's grey walls, and the laughter of its people" (IV.320). It is an essential part of her and one day she will proclaim herself Arya Stark once more.

> Polliver had stolen the sword from her when the Mountain's men took her captive, but when she and the Hound walked into the inn at the crossroads, there it was. The gods wanted me to have it. Not the Seven, nor Him of Many Faces, but her father's gods, the old gods of the north. The many-faced god can have the rest, she thought, but he can't have this. (IV.320)

Pyramids

Pyramids represent the pinnacle of manmade achievement. "The traditional square base represents earth, matter, form, and manifestation; the apex, heaven" (Shepherd 342). Meereen towers with them. Of course, Drogon the black dragon enjoys perching above them. As a creature of magic he's more than a match for the structures of man.

The 800-foot pyramid of Meereen was actually built for the fourth season. David Benioff comments:

> It just doesn't happen often anymore since more and more things are done with CG. But we've done these lavish huge sets and there something old Hollywood about that that I love. We have an incredible VFX team, the best in the world, and we rely on them for so many things. But for the actors there's something different about walking into a real environment and being in a room that has the power you're trying to convey. It's almost like the way cathedrals were designed to create awe. If you were a peasant and been working in fields your whole life and never seen a city, you'd walk into a cathedral for the first time and that's a religious experience – because you've never seen anything like this before. (Hibberd, "Showrunners")

Rose

House Tyrell is of course the house of roses, with a golden one on a green field. When golden roses first came to Europe, they symbolized jealousy and fading affection. A gift of such a rose meant the relationship was doomed. This seems a strong fit for Margaery. "In accordance with a very ancient custom dating as far back as the time of Pope Gregory I, the sending of a golden rose by the Pope to people of distinction is a symbol of special papal benediction" (Ferguson 38). In heraldry, the rose is a symbol of hope and joy. With red flowers, it is a symbol of grace, beauty, and sometimes martyrdom. It is also a sign of the seventh son (Mounet Lipp). As such, it's a logical token for unneeded third son Loras (in the books he has two older brothers). The martyrdom, however, may be the Tyrells' enemies rather than themselves.

Sansa wears pink roses around her collar for the Tournament of the Hand, and Loras throws her a red rose. Roses can represent romance, courtship, and virtue, and indeed, she nearly marries into House Tyrell to live in its beautiful gardens. By contrast, Olenna Tyrell is nicknamed Queen of Thorns for her sharp nature.

The other character associated with roses is Ned's sister Lyanna Stark, who loved blue roses beyond anything. Blue roses (along with their snowy cold imagery) symbolize the unattainable, and certainly Lyanna is beyond the reach of Robert, Rhaegar, and all who loved her. Daenerys's vision in the House of the Undying includes blue roses (Lyanna's favorite) blooming from an ice wall, a likely allusion to Lyanna's child at the Wall (II.515-516). .They have a wonderful scent, which many fans believe predicts a romance between her and Jon. It also parallels the book's legend of Bael the Bard and the blue rose, in which a Stark daughter is stolen from the family, only to give the House a son by her lover. Daario gives Daenerys a blue rose in "Two Swords" to acquaint her with the countryside. As she smiles, there is nonetheless a wide gulf between them.

Sacrifice

There will come a day after a long summer when the

stars bleed and the cold breath of darkness falls heavy on the world. In this dread hour a warrior shall draw from the fire a burning sword. And that sword shall be Lightbringer, the Red Sword of Heroes, and he who clasps it shall be Azor Ahai come again, and the darkness shall flee before him. (II.110) .

However, there's a dark side to the prophecy, as Salladhor Saan explains after:

Do you know the tale of the forging of Lightbringer? I shall tell it to you. It was a time when darkness lay heavy on the world. To oppose it, the hero must have a hero's blade, oh, like none that had ever been. And so for thirty days and thirty nights Azor Ahai labored sleepless in the temple, forging a blade in the sacred fires. Heat and hammer and fold, heat and hammer and fold, oh, yes, until the sword was done. Yet when he plunged it into water to temper the steel it burst asunder.

"Being a hero, it was not for him to shrug and go in search of excellent grapes such as these, so again he began. The second time it took him fifty days and fifty nights, and this sword seemed even finer than the first. Azor Ahai captured a lion, to temper the blade by plunging it through the beast's red heart, but once more the steel shattered and split. Great was his woe and great was his sorrow then, for he knew what he must do. "A hundred days and a hundred nights he labored on the third blade, and as it glowed white-hot in the sacred fires, he summoned his wife. 'Nissa Nissa' he said to her, for that was her name, 'bare your breast, and know that I love you best of all that is in this world.' She did this thing, why I cannot say, and Azor Ahai thrust the smoking sword through her living heart. It is said that her cry of anguish and ecstasy left a crack across the face of the moon, but her blood and her soul and her strength and her courage all went into the steel. Such is the tale of the forging of Lightbringer, the Red Sword of Heroes. (II.155)

.

Azor Ahai clearly must sacrifice his great love to become his world's champion. Many characters make sacrifices, but they don't appear to be enough. Melisandre and Stannis plot to execute Gendry (Edric Storm in the books) because he has king's blood. In book five, Melisandre plans further royal sacrifices.

> Further, Melisandre is eager to sacrifice those with a king's blood, as she pronounces: "The Lord of Light cherishes the innocent. There is no sacrifice more precious. From his king's blood and his untainted fire, a dragon shall be born" (III.724). In this case, it's almost easier to name characters who don't have king's blood: The Starks, Greyjoys, and most other great houses were kings before Aegon the Conqueror (some Houses died out and others were advanced in their places, so not every great house fits this description). There's everyone who's named themselves kings in recent years, including Mance Rayder. And all the bastards once again. Melisandre seems eager for innocents in particular, though it's unclear which factors do in fact make the best sacrifice. Her insistence on sacrificing royal children echoes Azor Ahai's sacrifice of a lion – powerful-looking, but not the required sacrifice of the heart. Once again, she seems misguided in her approach. (Frankel, *Winter is Coming*)

However, Stannis and Melisandre have missed the point of the story – that the chosen one must truly love the sacrifice. Stannis's only daughter Shireen, with blood of the dragon and blood of kings, seems a more likely candidate. Other characters have lost loved ones but mostly not by choice. The remaining Starks have lost many loved ones, but they didn't choose their loved ones' deaths. Almost every House has lost sons, and many are down to their final heirs.

Daenerys comes closer, by sacrificing her unborn child for her husband, then killing her husband and burning Mirri Maz Duur on the pyre. In the House of the Undying, she sees an image of what she's lost, not only child but the destined hero who was to come: She beholds "a tall lord with copper skin and silver-gold hair...beneath the banner of a fiery stallion, a burning city behind him" (II.706). .However, her prophecy describes three fires she must light – two more just as momentous are still ahead.

Salt

The Ironborn have a salt-based culture: the sea is livelihood, religion, means of war and transportation. They keep salt wives they take through conquest. The King of the Iron Islands is also called the King of Salt and Rock. The Dhampir drinks salt water and bathes in the sea, drowning his followers to dedicate them. During the reign of King Qhored, the Ironborn could rightfully claim that his writ ran "wherever men can smell salt water or hear the crash of waves."

Bread and salt are used to secure guest right, as they're a token of food, representing a full meal and the privilege of shelter. It was necessary for life and also valuable as a preservative. This is emphasized when Davos smuggles salt fish to Stannis's starving garrison along with the onions. Likewise, the "dosh khaleen," matriarchs of the Dothraki, receive "traditional gifts of salt, silver and seed" (I.587).

Salt is the symbol of strength and superiority. Christ, in the Sermon on the Mount, called His disciples 'the salt of the earth' [Matthew 5:13]. Since salt protects food from decay, it is sometimes used as a symbol of protection against evil and, in this context, is placed in the mouth of the child being baptized. There is a blessing for salt

which can be placed on a window sill or elsewhere to
ward off evil. (Ferguson 44)

Throughout the world, salt, a vital component of the body, is used for purification and to ward off evil.

There's also the prophecy "Azor Ahai shall be born again amidst smoke and salt to wake dragons out of stone." Renly on the show bursts out, "Born amidst salt and smoke... Is he a *ham*?" ("Garden of Bones"). While this is just silly, some fans wonder about the possibility of resurrection in the salting and smoking rooms below the Wall.

Seven

The series begins with seven Stark children (counting Theon and Jon) or with a family of seven, if the legitimate children and their parents are counted. They all soon scatter, until by the end of book two, none of the children see one another again (to date). Their perfect balance is destroyed, with enough dead (and confirmed dead) that they will never be seven once more.

Seven is "symbolic of perfect order, a complete period or cycle" (Cirlot 233). It's the number of musical notes, of colors in a rainbow, of the planetary spheres. As a combination of the feminine three and masculine four, it is perfectly balanced. The Seven Pointed Star of the New Gods combines square and triangle to make this union.

The seven-part New Gods who are different aspects of a single one are "similar to the concept of the Trinity in mainstream modern Christianity," one critic notes (Jones 112). Martin has said the same in interviews ("George R.R. Martin Interview,"). The gods are Maiden, Mother, Crone, Father, Smith, Warrior, Stranger. Notably, the female gods are life stages, while only one of the male gods is. One septon notes, "The Father rules, the Warrior fights, the Smith labors, and together they perform all that is rightful for a man" (IV.527). "Apparently, the lifecycle is 'all that is rightful' for a woman" (Frankel, *Women in Game of Thrones* 165). Meanwhile, the Stranger is considered androgynous, "less and more than human, unknown and unknowable" (II.372) representing the outsider and sometimes a personification of death.

Like Christians, the New Gods have seven hells. There are seven vices and seven virtues. An offended party can demand a trial of seven, a type of trial by combat. (The Andals believed that if seven champions fought on each side, the gods thus honored would be more likely to ensure justice.) Of course, many attempts to create this balance, with seven singers and seventy-seven courses at Joffrey's wedding, are more ostentatious than pious. The seven Kingsguard are appointed unwisely or fired abruptly just to fill the seven places. With no evidence the Seven have true power in Westeros, its people spend too much time in an empty show of sevens. The Targaryens worshipped the New Gods and were anointed by their High Septons, but by book's end, people may return to the Old Gods or the priests of R'hllor, both of which seem to be waking in the era of magic.

Perhaps coincidentally, there are Seven Kingdoms united as one country, also in a terrible imbalance as five kings lay claim to them. Melisandre was sold as "lot seven," but now is a follower of the One God, and has a new moral certainty in her fanaticism. By the story's end, the Seven Kingdoms may also join into one under their new savior.

Shadows

> No, Dany wanted to say, no, not that, you mustn't, but when she opened her mouth, a long wail of pain escaped, and the sweat broke over her skin. What was wrong with them, couldn't they see? Inside the tent the shapes were dancing, circling the brazier and the bloody bath, dark against the sandsilk, and some did not look human. She glimpsed the shadow of a great wolf, and another like a man wreathed in flames. (I.715)

The ancients believed a man's shadow could detach and go wandering, but "a living person's loss of shadow, however, was equated with the loss of the soul" (Walker 353). Above, Mirri Maz Duur conjures terrible shadows that obey her and aid her in her death magic.

Melisandre is known for birthing shadow creatures who kill Stannis's enemies, particularly his brother Renly.

> For many readers, it is not an image of fire but of shadow that represents Melisandre: First, the shadow of Stannis that crept into Renly's tent and assassinated him—a shadow with the power to slice through his gorget and cut his throat. Second, the shadow Davos witnesses when he rows Melisandre underneath the walls of Storm's End. Like the Wall, this ancient castle was built with powerful protective wards and her spells cannot cross the barrier. As soon as they pass under the walls, Melisandre is suddenly nine months pregnant and giving birth to a shadow; it crawls forth, as tall as a man, with Stannis's profile. (Scoble 136).

While shadows are generally associated with evil, Melisandre believes differently, emphasizing the ambiguous nature of magic:

> "Shadow?" Davos felt his flesh prickling. "A shadow is a thing of darkness."
> "You are more ignorant than a child, ser knight. There are no shadows in the dark. Shadows are the servants of light, the children of fire. The brightest flame casts the darkest shadows." (II.621-622) .

Asshai-by-the-Shadow is the source of the world's sorcerers, who deal in fire magic and death magic: Melisandre, Mirri Maz Duur, Quaithe of the Shadow. However, in this context, shadows may not be evil. Quaithe's advice to Daenerys has proved helpful:

> "To go north, you must go south. To reach the west, you must go east. To go forward you must go back, and to touch the light you must pass beneath the shadow."
> Asshai, Daenerys thought. She would have me go to Asshai. "Will the Asshai'i give me an army?" she demanded. "Will there be gold for me in Asshai? Will there be ships? What is there in Asshai that I will not find in Qarth?"
> "Truth," said the woman in the mask. And bowing, she faded back into the crowd. (II.426) .
>
> "So power is a mummer's trick?"
> "A shadow on the wall," Varys murmured, "yet shadows can kill. And ofttimes a very small man can cast a very large shadow." (II.132)

In Moqorro's vision later, Tyrion is described as a small man with a large shadow as he tries once more to influence events (V.436). Stannis is described in Daenerys's House of the Undying vision as having no shadow (certainly a shadow baby reference) ... perhaps he has less power than he believes.

Melisandre tells Jon: "Every man who walks the earth casts a shadow on the world. Some are thin and weak, others long and dark. You should look behind you, Lord Snow. The moon has kissed you and etched your shadow upon the ice twenty feet tall" (V.380). It's also interesting that the moon, a feminine symbol, has kissed him – perhaps the moon of Drogo's heart is coming for him.

Bran sees more menacing shadows around his own family, suggesting darkness and death will come for them.

> He saw his father pleading with the king, his face etched with grief. He saw Sansa crying herself to sleep at night, and he saw Arya watching in silence and holding her secrets hard in her heart. There were shadows all around them. One shadow was as dark as ash, with the terrible face of a hound. Another was armored like the sun, golden and beautiful. Over them both loomed a giant in armor made of stone, but when he opened his visor, there was nothing inside but darkness and thick black blood. (I.136-137)

> Based on the events of the series, the three shadows seem clear. The ash-dark shadow with the face of a hound is obviously the Hound, Sandor Clegane. In the golden armor is Jaime Lannister. Littlefinger's family sigil is a stone titan, and he's certainly a danger to Ned and Sansa. However, the giant in armor made of stone is more likely Gregor Clegane, the Mountain that Rides, based on his eventual fate with "darkness and thick black blood." Sandor torments Sansa and Arya, while Jaime's fight with Ned finally leads to his demise. Gregor Clegane fights for the Lannisters and devastates the Stark troops and the Tully countryside. In the second book, takes Arya prisoner for a time as well. (Frankel, "Winter is Coming")

Skulls

Skulls. A thousand skulls, and the bastard boy again. Jon

> Snow...
> The flames crackled softly, and in their crackling she
> heard the whispered name Jon Snow. His long face
> floated before her, limned in tongues of red and orange,
> appearing and disappearing again, a shadow half- seen
> behind a fluttering curtain. Now he was a man, now a
> wolf, now a man again. But the skulls were here as well,
> the skulls were all around him.
> Snowflakes swirled from a dark sky and ashes rose to
> meet them, the grey and the white whirling around each
> other as flaming arrows arced above a wooden wall and
> dead things shambled silent through the cold, beneath a
> great grey cliff where fires burned inside a hundred
> caves. Then the wind rose and the white mist came
> sweeping in, impossibly cold, and one by one the fires
> went out. Afterward only the skulls remained.
> Death, thought Melisandre. The skulls are death. (V.407-
> 408)

This symbolism seems clear enough as skulls surround Jon, and violence closes in around him. (Of course, his death is uncertain, and prophetic visions in the series are often twisted or misleading). In this glimpse, Melisandre is seeing Wildings and the Night Watch in the present, battling wights at Hardhome.

> Visions danced before her, gold and scarlet, flickering,
> forming and melting and dissolving into one another,
> shapes strange and terrifying and seductive. She saw the
> eyeless faces again, staring out at her from sockets
> weeping blood. Then the towers by the sea, crumbling as
> the dark tide came sweeping over them, rising from the
> depths. Shadows in the shape of skulls, skulls that turned
> to mist, bodies locked together in lust, writhing and rolling
> and clawing. Through curtains of fire great winged
> shadows wheeled against a hard blue sky. (V.407-408)

Skulls traditionally symbolize the transience of life or contemplation of death. Skulls turning to mist reinforces this imagery.

They also cover the lands of the Free Cities. "Ghis's legions were shattered in the final war. Its brick walls were pulled down, its streets and buildings were turned to ash and cinder by dragonflame, and its fields were sown with salt, sulfur, and skulls." The marketplace of Meereen features landmarks like the statue of the chainmaker and the spire of skulls.

Many important skulls have been seen in the series:

- The Targaryens' collection of dragon skulls
- Animal skulls surrounding Craster's keep
- The Children of the Forest line their halls with skulls
- Ser Ilyn's new sword with a skull on the pommel
- The skull delivered to Dorne that may or may not be genuine
- Piles of skulls brought to the Great Sept by the sparrows
- The Bridge of Skulls, location of one attack on the Wall, with perhaps another to come.
- Richard Lonmouth, Prince Rhaegar's squire, with a sigil of skulls and kisses (His family hasn't been mentioned since the Harrenhal tournament, so this is unlikely.)
- Rattleshirt, the wilding dressed in bones, and the replacement who wears his armor
- The Golden Company, who dip their dead commanders' skulls in gold and swear to bring them to Westeros.
- Seven Skulls, the Ironborn longship, though it's far to the east

Spear

The spear, shown in the Sunspear crest, suggests a mighty weapon but also the will of heaven. Many gods from Athena to Celtic solar heroes Lugh and Llew fought with spears (Shepherd 293). The Archangel Michael uses one as well. In the books, Oberyn wields a spear in combat, with poison on the tip. It is also a symbol of heraldry. "The spear, lance or spear-tipping is an emblem [of] the gallant service and devotion to the honor and chivalry" (Mounet Lipp). Oberyn is devoted to combat, and his niece Arianne relies on chivalry for her plans. Prince Doran of Dorne makes use of it as well. Of course the fact that treacherous Janos Slynt, who ruled the City Watch and betrayed Ned Stark, chooses a bloody spear as his sigil suggests many who follow chivalry truly have no honor. "A lordship and a castle for a spearthurst in the back, and you didn't even need to thrust the spear," Tyrion notes before banishing Slynt to the Wall (II.126). .

Stone

The Lightbringer prophecy states, "Azor Ahai shall be born again amidst smoke and salt to wake dragons out of stone." In the House of the Undying, Daenerys watches as "A great stone beast takes wing from a smoking tower, breathing shadow fire" (though she also dreams Robb eating supper with a wolf's head – the visions aren't all literal) (II.706). .Many characters are born again amidst smoke and salt, from their childhood birth to a near-death experience or rededication: Prince Rhaegar, Daenerys (twice!), Davos, Stannis, Jon (in book five), Bran (as Winterfell burns), Theon (in his dedication) and all his uncles.

Certainly, Daenerys literally wakes three dragons from stone, but many fans wonder if more dragons will awake from the eggs at Asshai or on Dragonstone.

"Let Theon your servant be born again from the sea, as you were. Bless him with salt, bless him with stone, bless him with steel." Salt, stone, and steel seem to be all the Ironmen have surrounding them, so this line may be a coincidence. But compared to the prophecy, it's quite close. Perhaps the Ironborn share the legend.

Dragons are substantially stone already: Tyrion examines the Targaryen dragon skulls and sees each is "black as onyx due to its high iron content." The teeth are "long, curving knives of black diamond" (I.121). Dany's eggs "shimmered like polished metal" and are heavy as stone (I.104). They cannot be damaged by fire. The isle of Dragonstone is predominately obsidian, shaped apparently by magic into fantastical dragon heads. Aside from the stone dragons on Dragonstone, there are stone crypts at Winterfell and frozen stone gargoyles as well.

Another interesting image is the stonemen, as they're called: people inflicted with greyscale. The disease, which scarred Shireen Baratheon's face and turned her partly to stone, is intriguing. By the fifth book, more characters with greyscale have appeared, some of whom may fulfill aspects of the prophecy. Stone represents proof against decay and death, as its durability brings a kind of immortality. This holds true for the crypts of Winterfell, with perhaps whatever mysterious proof of his parentage awaits Jon there. However, this is sadly ironic in the case of the Stonemen, with whom the "preservation" leads to death.

Stone is a bastard name given to people around the Eyrie including Alayne Stone (books 3-4), and Mya Stone (a Baratheon bastard in the books). The mountain clans Tyrion recruits include the Stone Crows. Lady Stoneheart seems to take her name not from them but from her new outlook. Likewise, Ned's maternal grandmother was a "Flint of the mountains" who loved to climb, as Bran does. Gregor "the Mountain" Clegane looks like "he was chiseled out of rock" (III.970), and Littlefinger's grandfather's shield bears the stony Titan of Braavos. Though most of these references are unlikely to touch the prophecy, by the fourth book, all the Stark children are hiding in stone one way or another, with Arya in a city that's "all stone, a grey city in a green sea" and Bran learning in a cave. Sansa calls herself a stone. Rickon finds his way to Skagos, where the Skagosi are known as the Stoneborn. Perhaps they will all emerge from hiding as dragons – a force to be feared.

Straw Men

The talisman Catelyn weaves in "Dark Wings, Dark Words" to protect her children is made of small straw figures on a twig frame. She makes it for Bran and Rickon, and then soon hears they've died despite her attempt. She mentions making them twice before, once to pray Bran would live and once for Jon Snow. Both times, her prayer for the child's survival was granted, but she found herself more unhappy than before. (This proves true a third time, as Bran and Rickon survive, but she thinks they've died.)

Poor Tommen jousts with a straw man and loses at Joffrey's nameday tournament. As such, he emphasizes his helplessness in the vicious world of King's Landing. By contrast, Arya can pulverize them. "Face, tits, balls – I hit 'em right where I wanted to," Arya proclaims after shooting at dummies. "Aye, but you took your sweet time of it. You won't be fighting straw men, little lady," a man of the Brotherhood Without Banners replies ("The Climb"). In fact, Arya has already killed men but will need to perfect her skills to be as powerful as she wishes.

Scarecrows appear on the Wall, as Jon and his friends hide behind decoys when the Wildlings attack. They begin naming the scarecrows after their dead and making bets on who will fall next. As the scarecrows increase but their men do not, Jon starts to despair. In both cases, straw men are only an illusion, unable to protect those still living.

Swords

"With their symbolic power over life and death, swords are considered by many cultures to be conductors of divine will" (Shepherd 292). They suggest godlike right and perfect justice. King Arthur proves his bloodline when he draws the sword from the stone. Similarly in Westeros, the king's sword began a Targaryen civil war, when the king bestowed it on his Blackfyre bastard son instead of his legitimate heir over a century back. Tywin Lannister fumes that his family has lost their ancestral Valyrian steel sword, Brightroar, for it confirms his family's status. He actually lowers himself enough to steal the Stark greatsword, Ice, to remake for his house. There's also Lightbringer, the sword Melisandre insists is needed for the great war to come:

.

Azor Ahai "called for his wife, Nissa Nissa, and asked her to bare her breast. He drove his sword into her breast, her soul combining with the steel of the sword, creating Lightbringer" (II.115). This moment must repeat for the great hero to live once again. Further, if Jon or Dany is the great hero, this could fulfill all three terms of the prophecy: If Azor reborn (many signs point to Jon) betrayed his one true love Daenerys and stabbed her to reforge Lightbringer (treason for love), the blade would blaze up in a mighty flame (fire for love), and Daenerys might even be trapped inside the sword as Nissa was, making it her mount for love. Her fire would make the sword a true Lightbringer, combining the love prophecies as the first three were combined. Of course, this would herald a grisly end to Daenerys if she couldn't return through some kind of magic or escape into an animal, her other possible mount for love. "Knowing" three treasons suggests they all will be betrayals of her, but she could be the betrayer and light a pyre under her own true love (whether Jon or someone else), kindling her fire to love as a wrenching sacrifice. Only life can pay for life, so it's certain the chosen one of Westeros will have a hard road. (Frankel, *Winter is Coming*)

Valyrian steel swords are needed to combat the Others (it appears). Valyrian steel is a combination of manmade steel and magic, a symbol of the forceful masculine world with a touch of the mystical. The sword, as well as being a physical symbol of death, is one of "the spirit and the word of God" (Cirlot 324). Knights are intended to use them to defend the righteous against darkness, while in alchemy swords represent purifying fire. There are many in Westeros and lost in the east, each significant. If three heroes riding three dragons will save the world from darkness, it's possible each will need a magic sword of ice, fire, or both.

One possibility for Lightbringer is the sword Oathkeeper,

which a greedy Tywin forges from Ned Stark's sword Ice into a new red Lannister sword, blending ice and fire. It's strangely smoke-stained, and has already killed Ned Stark – a serious sacrifice for the Stark children, but since none of them chose it (despite Sansa's tiny betrayal), this loss likely foreshadows another greater sacrifice to come. Given eventually to Brienne, it might easily pass to a Stark and become the Oathkeeper of Daenerys and her allies, protecting Westeros. Its brother, given to Joffrey and named Widow's Wail, has a similar potential. If three swords are needed, for the three-headed dragon of Daenerys and her partners, this pair could both be needed. (Frankel, *Winter is Coming*)

Showrunner Dan Weiss explained the significance of beginning season four with the reforging of Ned Stark's sword, Ice, saying, "Melting down Ice and subdividing it to the two swords happens off screen in the books, but it's something so strong about the image of this most iconic weapon we've had on the show and all it signifies for the Starks and family history seeing it literally melted down and re-purposed for Tywin's liking, it speaks volumes without saying a word" (Hibberd, "Maisie Williams").

Tywin explains in the books, "With this fool's jabber of Stannis and his magic sword, it seemed to me that we had best give Joffrey something extraordinary as well. A king should bear a kingly weapon (III.433). He appropriates Ned's weapon and molds it to his own purpose, just as he did with his daughter Sansa and his position as Hand. In the books, the color is indeed extraordinary: "Most Valyrian steel was a grey so dark it looked almost black, as was true here as well. But blended into the folds was a red as deep as the grey. The two colors lapped over one another without ever touching, each ripple distinct, like waves of night and blood upon some steely shore"

(III.434). Oathkeeper and Widow's Wail thus become swords of ice and fire, prepared for the conflict ahead.

Meanwhile, Jon has Longclaw, a gift from his commander and a sword of bear and wolf, appropriate for a warg. It's a sword of the North as well as animal magic, as House Mormont is sworn to House Stark and there are rumors they are shapeshifters. Brightroar, the ancestral sword of House Lannister, was lost in Valyria long ago. This name of course suggests the roar of flames as well as red and gold lions.

There are fabled Targaryen swords, now lost: Blackfyre, sword of Aegon the Conqueror, was "a fabled blade of Valyrian steel passed from king to king... until Aegon IV chose to bestow it on Daemon [his bastard son] instead of his legitimate son, Daeron...Some felt that the sword symbolized the monarchy, so the gift was the seed from which the Blackfyre Rebellions grew," Martin explains. ("So Spake Martin," C91 P90). The second Blackfyre rebellion failed as the hopeful king didn't have his father's sword. Its whereabouts are uncertain, but it may remain with the exiled Blackfyre descendants, the Golden Company. Martin promises more about the sword will reappear. The latest Targaryen claimant may have it, or Daenerys may come across it in the east.

Aegon the Conqueror's warrior sister fought with Dark Sister, which passed to the Targaryen king's bastard and Hand Bloodraven just after the Blackfyre rebellion. Arya specifically mentions it while serving as Tywin's page on the show, foreshadowing its importance. It may have traveled north with

Bloodraven when he took the black, and so pass to a Stark.

Melisandre gives Stannis Lightbringer, but her fellow Red Priest Thoros of Myr used to create flaming swords with cheap illusions. Gendry reports: "He'd just dip some cheap sword in wildfire and set it alight. It was only an alchemist's trick" (III.308). When Maester Aemon discovers the sword isn't hot, he seems to doubt its pedigree (compared to the sizzling horn from Asshai).

> There are other magical swords: Ser Arthur Dayne's fabled Dawn glows with a white light and was carved from a meteor (echoing the red comet!). It famously passes only to one who's worthy, echoing the Lightbringer legend. With the metaphor of morning ending the long night, it may have a part to play – Maester Aemon even calls the upcoming endless winter the "war for the dawn" (III.884). The Sword of the Morning is a constellation, as is the Ice Dragon – ice and fire are enacting their battle in the heavens (III.355). However, Dawn's owner died battling Ned Stark at the Tower of Joy and Ned (allegedly) took it to the Dayne castle, where it sits unused. It may have a link with Jon, his biological family, or his tale. However, its lack of mention after book two suggests a lack of importance. (Frankel, *Winter is Coming*)

With his head on a weirwood tree, Jaime dreams of swords. It's unclear if these will become literal:

> Jaime groped under the water until his hand closed upon the hilt. Nothing can hurt me so long as I have a sword. As he raised the sword a finger of pale flame flickered at the point and crept up along the edge, stopping a hand's breath from the hilt. The fire took on the color of the steel itself so it burned with a silvery-blue light, and the gloom pulled back. Crouching, listening, Jaime moved in a circle, ready for anything that might come out of the darkness. The water flowed into his boots, ankle deep

and bitterly cold. Beware the water, he told himself.
There may be creatures living in it, hidden deeps…
… The steel links parted like silk. "A sword," Brienne
begged, and there it was, scabbard, belt, and all. She
buckled it around her thick waist. The light was so dim
that Jaime could scarcely see her, though they stood a
scant few feet apart. In this light she could almost be a
beauty, he thought. In this light she could almost be a
knight. Brienne's sword took flame as well, burning
silvery blue. The darkness retreated a little more.
"The flames will burn so long as you live," he heard
Cersei call. "When they die, so must you." (III.610)

Will Jaime fight in the Battle for the Dawn, with a sword of
"blue light" and "pale flame"? Will Brienne? Or was this
dream simply that?

A crystal sword used by a White Walker looks like a
long icicle. When asked, Martin says an Other Sword is
made from "Ice. But not like regular old ice. The Others can
do things with ice that we can't imagine and make
substances of it" (Shaw). Obsidian spear points and knives
seem a logical counterpoint, called "dragonglass" and
formed from the fires of the earth. Still, a literal fire sword
remains a possibility in the great war to come.

Three

three heads has the dragon…
…three fires must you light…one for life and one for death
and one to love…
…three mounts must you ride…one to bed and one to
dread and one to love…
…three treasons will you know…once for blood and once
for gold and once for love…
(II.515).

This prophecy, given to Daenerys in the House of
the Undying, emphasizes her role as classic heroine.
It's a number of fairytales: three helpers, three

wishes, three sons. "Three symbolizes spiritual synthesis and is the formula for the creation of each of the worlds" (Cirlot 232). It thus makes a tale: birth, continuance, and death. Dany's three pattern will likely correspond to these last. The first set corresponds with the second: Daenerys's silver horse from her wedding and the fire that makes her Mother of Dragons. The second set may take place around the fifth book (or possibly in the next books to come –she rides a dragon and is betrayed many times, but the fire may not have been sufficiently significant). The third set, bound with love, will likely be the climax of the series for Daenerys, and may awaken warg powers and a lasting partnership...likely with Jon Snow, the ice to her fire.

Aegon the Conqueror had three dragons, one for him and two for his sister-wives and fellow conquerors. While courting Daenerys, Ser Jorah tells her that her dragons suggest she must take the same path – one mount for her and two for a pair of dragonrider husbands and partners. While it's unlikely she will choose Jorah to fill the role, Daenerys lives her life in threes: Three bloodriders with three special weapons. Three handmaids, first Doreah, Irri, and Jhiqui, then Doreah is replaced by Missandei in the books. And three dragon eggs that become three dragons.

Motifs of three sons are seen with Robert, Stannis, and Renly Baratheon, the three Tyrell sons (in the book), Theon and his dead brothers, and the three Stark boys (as well as the same-age trio of Jon, Robb, and Theon). There are three Lannister siblings and three Lannister children (through Cersei). Tywin likewise has two living siblings, Genna (a Frey by marriage) and Kevan. Doran Martell had two siblings, Elia and Oberyn, and he has three children, all caught in strategic marriage alliances.

Melisandre burns three leeches to bring about three deaths: Kings Robb, Balon Greyjoy, and Joffrey. There are also three red priests about: Melisandre, Thoros of Myr, and Quaithe. The trio that saves the world will likely be backed by a trio of magical advisors, as well as three swords, three dragons, and three destinies.

Towers

Towers, like pyramids, symbolize mankind's physical might and achievement as builders strain towards the sun. The Freys are represented by two grey towers and Ser Jorah weds a Hightower wife who's too greedy for him to support. Thus ambition turns to corruption in the series. Another notable tower is the Tower of the Hand, home to Jon Arryn, Ned Stark, Tyrion, and Tywin, before Cersei has it burned down out of anger and spite. None of these men have happy tenures as Hand.

Twins

Twins frequently represent the counterbalance of good and evil, with the twins set as enemies. Cersei and Jaime are treasonous partners in crime in the first season, though they evolve in different directions by the fourth – Jaime has learned morality and humility, while Cersei's cruelty and paranoia grow ever stronger.

Likewise, incest in itself symbolizes, according to Jung, the longing for union with the essence of one's own self. As Cersei says, "Targaryens wed brothers and sisters for 300 years to keep the bloodline pure. Jaime and I are more than brother and sister. We shared a womb. We came into this world together, we belong together" ("You Win Or You Die"). In a cruel world, with no mother and an unfeeling father, the twins cling to each other and symbolically, themselves.

Other brother-sister pairs are likewise a contrast of opposites. Arrogant, cruel Viserys is everything his sister is not – Daenerys, the true "child of the dragon" has real magic, and in time, real power as well. Meera Reed is all warrior, while her brother is mystic and teacher. Margaery is the crafty, clever sibling, while Loras seems to be a follower, of his family's dictates or his lover Renly's.

Underground

The cellars represent the subconscious, where hidden drives and impulses lurk. Varys is master of the deepest dungeons, where Maegor the Cruel hid his nastiest secrets. The Targaryen dragon skulls have been banished below the castle, but they remain there, awaiting the Targaryens' return. Meereen seems mighty, but its sewers are vulnerable. Several characters dream of cellars and what dwells there. As Jon explains:

> I'm walking down this long empty hall...opening doors, shouting names...the castle is always empty...the stables are full of bones. That always scares me. I start to run, then, throwing open doors, climbing the tower three steps at a time, screaming for someone, for anyone. And then I find myself in front of the door to the crypts. It's black inside, and I can see the steps spiraling down. Somehow I know I have to go down there, but I don't want to. I'm

> afraid of what might be waiting for me...I scream that I'm not a Stark, that this isn't my place, but it's no good, I have to go down anyway, so I start down, feeling the walls as I descend, with no torch to light the way. It gets darker and darker, until I want to scream...that's when I always wake. (I.224-225)

The secrets of his birth may be there waiting for him. Bran and Rickon emerge from the crypts alive and well, though it's notable Hodor is frightened of them at the end of book two. Martin writes, "Hodor was only afraid of the crypts =at that specific time= Not before and not after," leading many to wonder if something was awakened there ("So Spake Martin, C91, P255).

Jaime lays his head on a weirwood tree and has a dream of all his guilty secrets buried underground.

> They gave no answer, only prodded him with the points of their spears. He had no choice but to descend. Down a twisting passageway he went, narrow steps carved from the living rock, down and down. I must go up, he told himself. Up, not down. Why am I going down? Below the earth his doom awaited, he knew with the certainty of dream; something dark and terrible lurked there, something that wanted him. Jaime tried to halt, but their spears prodded him on. If only I had my sword, nothing could harm me. The steps ended abruptly on echoing darkness. Jaime had the sense of vast space before him. He jerked to a halt, teetering on the edge of nothingness. A spearpoint jabbed at the small of the back, shoving him into the abyss. He shouted, but the fall was short. He landed on his hands and knees, upon soft sand and shallow water. There were watery caverns deep below Casterly Rock, but this one was strange to him. "What place is this?"
> "Your place." The voice echoed; it was a hundred voices, a thousand, the voices of all the Lannisters since Lann the Clever, who'd lived at the dawn of days. But most of all it was his father's voice, and beside Lord Tywin stood

> his sister, pale and beautiful, a torch burning in her hand. Joffrey was there as well, the son they'd made together, and behind them a dozen more dark shapes with golden hair.
> "Sister, why has Father brought us here?"
> "Us? This is your place, Brother. This is your darkness."
> (III.610)

The Kingsguard surrounds him there and reminds him of the oaths he betrayed. Thus the underground symbolizes all he's repressed, but also the family who remains a part of him, all the voices inside his head.

In the North, Bran must journey underground into the caves below the weirwoods. The three-eyed crow tells him: "The strongest trees are rooted in the dark places of the earth. Darkness will be your cloak, your shield, your mother's milk. Darkness will make you strong" (V.450). As he learns, he lives in the subconscious of the world, a place of forgotten peoples where secrets are free for taking, using the power of the weirwoods.

Valar Morghulis

"Valar Morghulis" (All Men Must Die) say the Faceless Men. Jaqen H'ghar gives Arya the password – if she says it to a Faceless Man and gives him her iron coin, she can join them in Braavos. The counter words are Valar Dohaeris – all men must serve.

Martin says the Faceless Men have existed for "Thousands of years, if their traditions can be believed. Longer than Braavos itself" and that "their interests go further, they originated in Valyria before the fall, and their core organizing principle is religious" ("So Spake Martin" C435, P540). Braavos believes in many gods, but all are believed to be aspects of the Many-Faced God. "In Qohor he is the

Black Goat, in Yi Ti, the Lion of Night, in Westeros, the Stranger" (IV.507). Arya's teacher Syrio echoes this when he says, "There is only one god, and his name is Death. And there is only one thing we say to Death: 'Not today.'" Their words are interesting in context of the show, as the wights refuse to die – perhaps killing them and making sure "all men die" was once the Faceless Men's mission. It's also possible they will turn on the Red Priests or Qyburn, the ones who have resuscitated people from death. The Faceless Men are eventually seen meddling in the Maesters' Citadel in Oldtown, possibly looking for books of lore. They may finally join the war...but on which side?

The Wall

Men of the Night's Watch have always guarded the Southern lands, not from wildings, who are men like any other, but from White Walkers. The Wall itself has the ancient magic of the weirwoods, allowing none but rangers to pass. The oath explains:

> Night gathers, and now my watch begins. It shall not end until my death. I shall take no wife, hold no lands, father no children. I shall wear no crowns and win no glory. I shall live and die at my post. I am the sword in the darkness. I am the watcher on the walls. I am the fire that burns against the cold, the light that brings the dawn, the horn that wakes the sleepers, the shield that guards the realms of men. I pledge my life and honor to the Night's Watch, for this night and all the nights to come. (I.522)

While the horn part is literally true, the Watch is supposed to fight White Walkers with fire and light, though they've only just started remembering that. Valyrian steel and dragonglass, mostly gone from the world, are the magical weapons that will aid them.

These appear to work better by the Wall than anywhere else. In fact, Melisandre's magic is stronger at the Wall (V.411). Daenerys's dragons and the Stark shapeshifting may gain strength there as well.

> Early in A Game of Thrones, we also see the architectural wonder of the Wall, a great monument of ice and stone approximately three hundred miles long and seven hundred feet high. Stories say Bran the Builder engineered the Wall, eight thousand years past, weaving spells of protection into it to shield Westeros from the Others and monstrosities from the Lands of Always Winter. Stories tell that magic is the only way to bring down the Wall, as well. The Horn of Winter, or the Horn of Joramun, is an artifact that the wildlings say can not only bring down the Wall, but awaken the giants (Scoble 127).

In the third season, Jon and his Wildling friends climb the 700-foot Wall. As they do, Littlefinger gives a speech linking the climb with power: "Chaos isn't a pit. Chaos is a ladder. Many who try to climb it fail and never get to try again. The fall breaks them. And some are given a chance to climb, but they refuse. They cling to the realm or the gods or love. Illusions. Only the ladder is real. The climb is all there is" ("The Climb"). While Jon's climb is meant to defend the realm, many other characters "climb" to reach their ambitions and indeed are destroyed or refuse to try.

Water Gardens

More than anything, Prince Doran of Dorne enjoys watching children play in the Water Gardens.

> "I am eager to see [Myrcella] once again," said Ser Balon. "And to visit your Water Gardens. I've heard they are very beautiful."
> "Beautiful and peaceful," the prince said. "Cool

breezes, sparkling water, and the laughter of
children. The Water Gardens are my favorite place in this
world, ser. One of my ancestors had them built to please
his Targaryen bride and free her from the dust and heat
of Sunspear. Daenerys was her name. She was sister to
King Daeron the Good, and it was her marriage that
made Dorne part of the Seven Kingdoms. The whole
realm knew that the girl loved Daeron's bastard brother
Daemon Blackfyre, and was loved by him in turn, but the
king was wise enough to see that the good of thousands
must come before the desires of two, even if those two
were dear to him. It was Daenerys who filled the gardens
with laughing children. Her own children at the start, but
later the sons and daughters of lords and landed knights
were brought in to be companions to the boys and girls of
princely blood. And one summer's day when it was
scorching hot, she took pity on the children of her grooms
and cooks and serving men and invited them to use the
pools and fountains too, a tradition that has endured till
this day." (V.505)

Prince Doran shut his eyes and opened them again.
Hotah could see his leg trembling underneath the
blanket. "If you were not my brother's daughters, I would
send the three of you back to your cells and keep you
there until your bones were grey. Instead I mean to take
you with us to the Water Gardens. There are lessons
there if you have the wit to see them."
"Lessons?" said Obara. "All I've seen are naked
children."
"Aye," the prince said. "I told the story to Ser Balon,
but not all of it. As the children splashed in the pools,
Daenerys watched from amongst the orange trees, and a
realization came to her. She could not tell the high-born
from the low. Naked, they were only children. All
innocent, all vulnerable, all deserving of long life, love,
protection. "There is your realm," she told her son and
heir, "remember them, in everything you do." My own
mother said those same words to me when I was old
enough to leave the pools. (V.510)

This is a theme of the series – that more innocents die in war than the deserving do. Certainly, Doran mourns his younger siblings. His long campaign appears designed to saves innocent lives and achieve a lasting peace, though his daughter and the Sand Snakes are more eager to shed the blood of Joffrey's siblings Tommen and Myrcella. As Arianne Martell considers seeking the throne in her own right and the Sand Snakes set forth to scheme and murder, it's clear the Dornish will spill blood in the sixth book.

Weddings

> Varys: I've always hated the bells. They ring for horror, a dead king, a city under siege.
> Tyrion: A wedding.
> Varys: Exactly. ("Blackwater")

Robb and Talisa are wed in season two, quietly and humbly in the forest. They have a happy union, though their marriage insults the Freys and dooms Robb's campaign.

Book three has majestic, pompous weddings: Sansa and Tyrion, the Red Wedding, and Joffrey's royal wedding. "A royal wedding is not an amusement. A royal wedding is history – the time has come for us to contemplate our history," Joffrey says ("The Lion and the Rose"). A wedding is also meant to signify a joining of the souls, a perfect alliance and mixing of male and female. All the weddings of the series, however, are tinged with tragedy – either the emotions are tinged with sorrow and/or there are deaths at or just after the wedding. "War is war, but killing a man at a wedding... horrid. What sort of monster would do such a thing?" Olenna Tyrell asks

("The Lion and the Rose"). In fact, if the wedding signifies an alliance, as medieval wedding often did, murdering people at a wedding is a way of showing contempt and spitting on that very union. The Dothraki offer Dany and Drogo a joyous wedding, though here too, "A Dothraki wedding without at least three deaths is deemed a dull affair" (I.103).

In season four, Joffrey is married in cloth-of-gold with a thick black sash. Baratheon colors and royal colors, but that much yellow comes across as a sickly color, and the strong black suggests mourning or tragedy.

Margaery's gown at the wedding feast is white with gray vines. She wears a small stag crown with prominent roses, affirming her Baratheon alliance. Joffrey's crown in turn is a stag crown with rosebuds intertwined. The Tyrells of course are twining themselves deeper into the Baratheon ruling family. The dark vines and sharp thorns creep over Margaery's white wedding gown, marring its otherwise perfect whiteness (she almost certainly is not a maiden as she claims). Its bare arms and plunging neckline appear more deliberately provocative than vulnerable. The twisting vines also suggest the poison that kills Joffrey, known as the strangler.

What is Dead Will Never Die
While this seems like a pious phrase repeated by the Ironborn it's literally true. Lady Stoneheart, the Frankenstein-esque monster Robert Strong, and Beric Dondarrion return from death, as do the wights and the mysterious Coldhands. Baby Aegon Targaryen is

rumored to have returned from death, as have the last of the rebellious Blackfyres. Varamyr Sixskins, Orell, and other wargs have the power to live on in one of their animals, at least for a time, after their human body is killed.

Ghosts fill the world of Westeros: Six hundred years ago, Hardhome exploded north of the Wall. The "screaming caves" nearby seem to be "haunted by ghouls and demons and burning ghosts" (V.522). Harrenhal is said to be under a curse and haunted by the many ghosts there. Jaime Lannister thinks that in three hundred years, it's seen more horrors than Casterly Rock has in three thousand. When (in the books) Loras's brother wears Renly's armor to frighten Stannis's troops at the Blackwater, they believe in him, certain he's returned for revenge.

Many characters identify with ghosts, as Jon thinks, "The castle is a shell...not Winterfell, but the ghost of Winterfell" after the Starks are gone (V.471). Beric Dondarrion has actually returned from the dead and sees himself as another ghost:

> Sandor Clegane: King Robert is dead, Ned Stark is dead; my brother is alive. You all fight for ghosts.
> Beric Dondarrion: Oh, but that's what we are, ghosts. Waiting for you in the dark; you can't see us...but we see you. No matter whose cloak you wear; Lannister, Stark, Baratheon, you prey on the weak...The Brotherhood without Banners will hunt you down! ("And Now his Watch is Ended")

Upon the stillbirth of her child, Mirri Maz Duur advises Dany that Drogo will return from his comatose state. "When the sun rises in the west and sets in the east. When the seas go dry and mountains blow in the wind like leaves. When your womb quickens again, and you bear a living child. Then he will return, and not before."

> This may be a curse – a complex way of saying "never." Or as some fans note, it may have come true in the fifth book. The sun likely refers to the Martell sigil of a sun and spear and Quentyn Martell's story in *A Dance with Dragons*. During Daenerys's final chapter in the book, she notes that the Dothraki Sea is drying up in the onrushing autumn. The mountain-shaped pyramids of her city burn down and blow away in the wind. And she bleeds for the first time since she met Khal Drogo...It's either menstruation or a miscarriage, either way suggesting she can become pregnant now. Drogo has already returned in the form of her dragon, his namesake. Or something more literal or in a dream state may occur, now that Daenerys is prepared to bear a living child. When asked if Daenerys is fertile again, Martin comments only, "I am sure Daenerys would like to know. Prophecy can be a tricky business." (C91, P60) (Frankel, *Winter is Coming*)

Likewise, people's secrets never "stay buried" as Jon Arryn's death or the plans of the Dornish are revealed after several books. The people themselves, even the dead ones, are massive rallying points as Oberyn is determined to avenge his sister Elia or King Robert loves dead Lyanna more than his living wife. Jon Snow dreams that a secret is buried in Winterfell's crypts for him, and Bran and Rickon rise from the crypts unharmed. More returns are likely as the series continues.

The series itself follows the same pattern as an obscure fantasy series from the nineties becomes the world-changing blockbuster of 2011. Just as his series is forever transformed by its re-creation, so too are fans as they compete in the age-old struggle of the Game of Thrones.

APPENDIX
Actors and Creators

George R.R. Martin – Author
David Benioff – Executive Producer
D.B. Weiss – Executive Producer

Starring
Aidan Gillen as Lord Petyr Baelish
Alfie Allen as Theon Greyjoy
Carice van Houten as Lady Melisandre
Charles Dance as Tywin Lannister
Emilia Clarke as Daenerys Targaryen
Gwendoline Christie as Brienne of Tarth
Harry Lloyd as Prince Viserys Targaryen
Iain Glen as Ser Jorah Mormont
Isaac Hempstead-Wright as Bran Stark
Jack Gleeson as Joffrey Baratheon
Jason Momoa as Khal Drogo
Joe Dempsie as Gendry
John Bradley as Samwell Tarly
Kit Harrington as Jon Snow
Lena Headey as Queen Cersei Lannister
Liam Cunningham as Ser Davos Seaworth
Maisie Williams as Arya Stark
Mark Addy as King Robert Baratheon
Michelle Fairley as Catelyn Stark
Natalie Dormer as Margaery Tyrell

Nikolaj Coster-Waldau as Jaime Lannister
Oona Chaplin as Queen Talisa Stark
Peter Dinklage as Tyrion Lannister
Richard Madden as Robb Stark
Rose Leslie as Ygritte
Sophie Turner as Sansa Stark
Rory McCann as Sandor Clegane
Sean Bean as Lord Eddard Stark
Stephen Dillane as King Stannis Baratheon

Guest Starring
Aimee Richardson as Myrcella Baratheon
Amrita Acharia as Irri
Andy Beckwith as Rorge
Andy Kellegher as Polliver
Anton Lesser as Qyburn
Art Parkinson as Rickon Stark
Ben Crompton as Eddison Tollett
Ben Hawkey as Hot Pie
Callum Wharry as Tommen Baratheon
Charlotte Hope as Myranda
Ciarán Hinds as Mance Rayder
Clive Russell as Ser Brynden Tully
Conleth Hill as Lord Varys
Daniel Portman as Podrick Payne
Dean-Charles Chapman as Tommen Baratheon (season 4)
Diana Rigg as Lady Olenna Tyrell
Ed Skrein as Daario Naharis
Elizabeth Webster as Fat Walda Frey
Ellie Kendrick as Meera Reed
Esme Bianco as Ros
Finn Jones as Loras Tyrell
Gemma Whelan as Yara Greyjoy
Hafþór Júlíus Björnsson as Ser Gregor Clegane (season 4)
Hannah Murray as Gilly
Jerome Flynn as Bronn
Ian Beattie as Ser Meryn Trant

Ian McElhinney as Ser Barristan Selmy
Indira Varma as Ellaria Sand
Iwan Rheon as Ramsay Snow
Jacob Anderson as Grey Worm
James Cosmo as Jeor Mormont
Joel Fry as Hizdahr zo Loraq
Josef Altin as Pyp
Julian Glover as Grand Maester Pycelle
Kate Dickie as Lady Lysa Arryn
Kristian Nairn as Hodor
Kristofer Hivju as Tormund Giantsbane
Lino Facioli as Lord Robin Arryn
Luke Barnes as Rast
Mackenzie Crook as Orell
Maisie Dee as Daisy
Mark Gatiss as Tycho Nestoris
Mark Stanley as Grenn
Mia Soteriou as Mirri Maz Duur
Michael McElhatton as Lord Roose Bolton
Michiel Huisman as Daario Naharis (season 4)
Natalia Tena as Osha
Nathalie Emmanuel as Missandei
Noah Taylor as Locke
Paul Bentley as the High Septon
Paul Kaye as Thoros of Myr
Pedro Pascal as Prince Oberyn Martell
Pixie Le Knot as Kayla
Richard Dormer as Lord Beric Dondarrion
Richard Doubleday as Ser Vance Corbray
Roger Ashton-Griffiths as Lord Mace Tyrell
Ron Donachie as Ser Rodrik Cassel
Rupert Vansittart as Lord Yohn Royce
Sibel Kekilli as Shae
Thomas Brodie-Sangster as Jojen Reed
Tobias Menzies as Lord Edmure Tully
Tony Way as Dontos Hollard
Yuri Kolokolnikov as Styr, the Magnar of Thenn

SYMBOLS IN GAME OF THRONES

Episode List

		Episode Title	Director	Writers
1	1	"Winter Is Coming"	Tim Van Patten	David Benioff & D. B. Weiss
2	2	"The Kingsroad"	Tim Van Patten	David Benioff & D. B. Weiss
3	3	"Lord Snow"	Brian Kirk	David Benioff & D. B. Weiss
4	4	"Cripples, Bastards, and Broken Things"	Brian Kirk	Bryan Cogman
5	5	"The Wolf and the Lion"	Brian Kirk	David Benioff & D. B. Weiss
6	6	"A Golden Crown"	Daniel Minahan	Jane Espenson, David Benioff & D. B. Weiss
7	7	"You Win or You Die"	Daniel Minahan	David Benioff & D. B. Weiss
8	8	"The Pointy End"	Daniel Minahan	George R. R. Martin
9	9	"Baelor"	Alan Taylor	David Benioff & D. B. Weiss

10	10	"Fire and Blood"	Alan Taylor	David Benioff & D. B. Weiss
Season Two				
11	1	"The North Remembers"	Alan Taylor	David Benioff & D. B. Weiss
12	2	"The Night Lands"	Alan Taylor	David Benioff & D. B. Weiss
13	3	"What Is Dead May Never Die"	Alik Sakharov	Alik Sakharov
14	4	"Garden of Bones"	David Petrarca	Vanessa Taylor
15	5	"The Ghost of Harrenhal"	David Petrarca	David Benioff & D. B. Weiss
16	6	"The Old Gods and the New"	David Nutter	Vanessa Taylor
17	7	"A Man Without Honor"	David Nutter	David Benioff & D. B. Weiss
18	8	"The Prince of Winterfell"	Alan Taylor	David Benioff & D. B. Weiss
19	9	"Blackwater"	Neil Marshall	George R. R. Martin
20	10	"Valar Morghulis"	Alan Taylor	David Benioff & D. B. Weiss
Season Three				
21	1	"Valar Dohaeris"	Daniel Minahan	David Benioff & D. B. Weiss
22	2	"Dark Wings, Dark Words"	Daniel Minahan	Vanessa Taylor

23	3	"Walk of Punishment"	David Benioff	David Benioff & D. B. Weiss
24	4	"And Now His Watch Is Ended"	Alex Graves	David Benioff & D. B. Weiss
25	5	"Kissed by Fire"	Alex Graves	Bryan Cogman
26	6	"The Climb"	Alik Sakharov	David Benioff & D. B. Weiss
27	7	"The Bear and the Maiden Fair"	Michelle MacLaren	George R. R. Martin
28	8	"Second Sons"	Michelle MacLaren	David Benioff & D. B. Weiss
29	9	"The Rains of Castamere"	David Nutter	David Benioff & D. B. Weiss
30	10	"Mhysa"	David Nutter	David Benioff & D. B. Weiss

Season Four

31	1	"Two Swords"	Daniel Minahan	David Benioff & D. B. Weiss
32	2	"The Lion and the Rose"	Alex Graves	George R. R. Martin
33	3	"Breaker of Chains"	Alex Graves	David Benioff & D. B. Weiss
34	4	"Oathkeeper"	Michelle MacLaren	Bryan Cogman
35	5	"First of His Name"	Michelle MacLaren	David Benioff & D. B. Weiss

36	6	"The Laws of Gods and Men"	Alik Sakharov	Bryan Cogman
37	7	"Mockingbird"	Alik Sakharov	George R. R. Martin
38	8	"The Mountain and the Viper"	Alex Graves	David Benioff & D. B. Weiss
39	9	"The Watchers on the Wall"	Neil Marshall	David Benioff & D. B. Weiss
40	10	"The Children"	Alex Graves	David Benioff & D. B. Weiss

A Song of Ice and Fire Bibliography

A Song of Ice and Fire Novels
A Game of Thrones, Bantam Books, 1996
A Clash of Kings, Bantam Books, 1999
A Storm of Swords, Bantam Books, 2000
A Feast for Crows, Bantam Books, 2005
A Dance with Dragons, Bantam Books, 2011
The Winds of Winter, forthcoming/Bantam Books
A Dream of Spring, forthcoming/Bantam Books

A Song of Ice and Fire Short Stories
Dunk and Egg:
"The Hedge Knight" (1998) available in George R.R. Martin,
     Dreamsongs: Volume I (Bantam Books, 2012)
"The Sworn Sword" (2003) available in George R.R. Martin,
     Dreamsongs: Volume II (Bantam Books, 2012)
"The Mystery Knight" (2010) available in *Warriors,* edited
     by George R.R. Martin and Gardner Dozois. Tor Books,
     2010.
"The She-Wolves of Winterfell" Planned for inclusion in
     Dangerous Women, now delayed and instead intended
     for a forthcoming Dunk and Egg collection.

Other
"The Princess and the Queen," (novella about the
Targaryen Civil War called "The Dance of the
Dragons") *Dangerous Women,* edited by George R.R. Martin
and Gardner Dozois. USA: Tor Books, 2013. 703-784.

A Song of Ice and Fire Adaptations

A Game of Thrones: The Graphic Novel Series by Daniel Abraham (Adapter), George R.R. Martin (Author) and Tommy Patterson (Illustrator). Bantam Books. Ongoing.

The World of Ice and Fire: The Official History of Westeros and The World of A Game of Thrones by George R.R. Martin, Elio Garcia, and, Linda Antonsson. Bantam Books, 2014

The Lands of Ice and Fire (Poster Map) George R.R. Martin 2012.

A Game of Thrones (strategy board game) Fantasy Flight Games. 2003 (several expansions).

Game of Thrones: The Card Game Fantasy Flight Games. 2002 (many expansion decks).

A Game of Thrones (RPG) Guardians of Order/White Wolf Games 2006.

Works Cited

Game of Thrones: The Complete First Season. HBO Home Entertainment, 2012. DVD.

Game of Thrones: The Complete Second Season. HBO Home Entertainment, 2013. DVD.

Game of Thrones: The Complete Third Season. HBO Go. 2013. Online Television. http://www.hbogo.com.

"George R.R. Martin Interview," The World Science Fiction and Fantasy Convention, Aug 29-Sept 3 2012, in Chicago, IL.

Hibberd, James. "'Game of Thrones' premiere: Showrunners, Maisie Williams on Arya's dark twist" *EW* 6 Apr 2014. http://insidetv.ew.com/2014/04/06/game-of-thrones-premiere-aryas-interview/

--. "'Game of Thrones': This Showrunners Q&A Will Get You Really Excited for Season 4." *EW* 4 Apr 2014. http://insidetv.ew.com/2014/04/04/game-of-thrones-showrunners-season-4/

Martin, George R.R. *A Clash of Kings.* USA: Bantam Books, 1999.

--. "Correspondence with Fans." *The Citadel: So Spake Martin* http://www.westeros.org/Citadel/SSM.

--. *A Dance with Dragons.* USA: Bantam Books, 2011.

--. *A Feast for Crows.* USA: Bantam Books, 2005.

--. *A Game of Thrones.* USA: Bantam Books, 1996.

--. "The Hedge Knight" *Legends.* Ed. Robert Silverberg. USA: Tor, 1998. 451-534.

--. "Interview in Barcelona." *Asshai.com,* July 28, 2012. http://www.westeros.org/Citadel/SSM/Entry/Asshai.com_Interview_in_Barcelona.

--. "The Mystery Knight" *Warriors.* Ed. George R.R. Martin and Gardner Dozois. New York: Tor, 2010. 649-736.

--. "The Princess and the Queen," *Dangerous Women*, edited by George R.R. Martin and Gardner Dozois. New York: Tor, 2013. 703-784.

--. *A Storm of Swords,* USA: Bantam Books, 2000.

Prudom, Laura. "Game Of Thrones' Season 3: George R. R. Martin On Writing 'The Bear And The Maiden Fair' And 'The Winds Of Winter,'" *Huffington Post,* Mar 20 2013. http://www.huffingtonpost.com/2013/03/20/game-of-thrones-season-3-george-r-r-martin_n_2915069.html

Roberts, Josh. "'Game of Thrones' Exclusive! George R.R. Martin Talks Season Two, 'The Winds of Winter,' and Real-World Influences for 'A Song of Ice and Fire'" *Smarter Travel* 1 sApr 2012. http://www.smartertravel.com/blogs/today-in-travel/game-of-thrones-exclusive-george-martin-talks-season-the-winds-of-winter-and-real-world-influences-for-song-of-ice-and-fire.html?id=10593041

Shaw, Robert. "Interview with the Dragon" 2003. http://web.archive.org/web/20051103091500/nrctc.edu/fhq/vol1iss3/00103009

Vanity Fair. "George R.R. Martin Has a Detailed Plan For Keeping the Game of Thrones TV Show From Catching Up To Him" *Vanity Fair* 14 Mar 2014.

http://www.vanityfair.com/vf-hollywood/george-r-r-martin-interview?mbid=social_fbshare

"A Very Long Interview with George R.R. Martin," *Oh No They Didn't.com*, Oct 10 2012. http://ohnotheydidnt.livejournal.com/72570529.html.

Vineyard, Jennifer. *"Game of Thrones'* Natalie Dormer on Power Plays and the Margaery-Joffrey Dynamic" *Vulture 22 Apr 20*13. http://www.vulture.com/2013/04/game-of-thrones-margaery-natalie-dormer-interview.html

Secondary Sources

Andrews, Tamra, Editor. *Nectar and Ambrosia: An Encyclopedia of Food in World Mythology*. ABC-CLIO: Santa Barbara, CA, 2000.

Cogman, Bryan. *Inside HBO's Game of Thrones*. USA: Chronicle Books, 2012.

Cox, Edward. "Magic, Knowledge, and Metaphysics in *A Game of Thrones*." Jacoby 129-141.

Davidson, H.R. Ellis. *Myths and Symbols in Pagan Europe: Early Scandinavian and Celtic Religions*. Syracuse University Press: Syracuse, NY, USA, 1988.

Duval, R. Shannon. "The Things I Do For Love: Sex, Lies, and Game Theory." Jacoby 250-263.

Ferguson, George and George Wells Ferguson. *Signs & Symbols in Christian Art*. Oxford: Oxford University Press, 1959.

"The Food Code of Ice and Fire" *A Forum of Ice and Fire*. 16 Aug 2013 http://asoiaf.westeros.org/index.php/topic/95101-the-food-code-of-ice-and-fire/

Fox-Davies, A.C. *The Art of Heraldry: An Encyclopedia*

of Armory. U.K.: Bloomsbury Books 1986.

Frankel, Valerie Estelle. *Women in Game of Thrones.* Jefferson, NC: McFarland and Co., 2014.

– . *Winning the Game of Thrones: The Host of Characters and their Agendas.* USA: LitCrit Press, 2013.

– . *Winter is Coming: Symbols and Hidden Meanings in A Game of Thrones.* USA: Thought Catalogue, 2013.

Frost, Robert. "Fire and Ice," PoemHunter.com, 2003. http://www.poemhunter.com/poem/fire-and-ice.

"Game of Thrones: A Feminist Episode, a Gay Episode, or a Dull Episode?" *The Atlantic* 7 Apr 2013. http://www.theatlantic.com/entertainment/archive/2013/04/-i-game-of-thrones-i-a-feminist-episode-a-gay-episode-or-a-dull-episode/274734/

Geoffrey of Monmouth. *The History of the Kings of Britain.* Ed. and Trans. J. A. Giles. 1848. The Camelot Project. http://d.lib.rochester.edu/camelot.

Geoghegan, Eddie. "The 'Meaning' of Coats of Arms." Heraldry.ws. http://www.heraldry.ws/info/article05.html

Goguen, Stacy "'There Are No True Knights': The Injustice of Chivalry." Jacoby 205-219.

Heinz, Sabine. *Celtic Symbols.* USA: Sterling Publishing Company, 2008.

Henderson, George. *Survivals in Belief Among the Celts.* London: Macmillan and Co., 1911. The Sacred Texts Archive. http://www.sacred-texts.com.

Higginson, Thomas Wentworth. *Tales of the Enchanted Islands of the Atlantic.* New York: Grosset & Dunlap, 1898. The Sacred Texts Archive. http://www.sacred-texts.com/earth/teia.

Jacoby, Henry. "No One Dances the Water Dance."
Jacoby 236-249.
Jacoby, Henry, ed. *Game of Thrones and Philosophy:
Logic Cuts Deeper Than Swords.* USA: John Wiley &
Sons, 2012.
Jones, Andrew Zimmerman. "Of Direwolves and
Gods." Lowder 107-122.
Kistler, Alan. *The Unofficial Game of Thrones
Cookbook.* USA: F&W Media, 2012.
Lowder, James. "Introduction: In Praise of Living
History." Lowder xiii-xviii.
Lowder, James, ed. *Beyond the Wall: Exploring George
R. R. Martin's A Song of Ice and Fire.* USA: BenBella
Books, 2012.
Mounet Lipp, Gerhard and Bambi. "ML Mural Art."
Family Trees and Crests.
http://www.familytreesandcrests.com/heraldry-
symbols.htm
Scoble, Jesse. "A Sword without a Hilt: The Dangers of
Magic in (and to) Westeros." Lowder 123-140.
Shepherd, Rowena and Rupert. *1000 Symbols.* New
York: The Ivy Press, 2002.
Vinycomb, John. *Symbolic Creatures in Art with Special
Reference to the Use in British Heraldry.* London:
Chapman and Hall, Ltd. 1909. The Sacred Texts
Archive. http://www.sacred-texts.com.
Vizzini, Ned. "Beyond the Ghetto." Lowder 203-218.
Walker, Barbara G. *The Woman's Dictionary of Symbols
and Sacred Objects.* San Francisco: Harper, 1988.
Westfahl, Gary. "Back to the Egg" Lowder 53-72.

SYMBOLS IN GAME OF THRONES

Index

251

SYMBOLS IN GAME OF THRONES

About the Author

Valerie Estelle Frankel is the author of many nonfiction books:

- *Buffy and the Heroine's Journey*
- *From Girl to Goddess: The Heroine's Journey in Myth and Legend*
- *Katniss the Cattail: An Unauthorized Guide to Names and Symbols in The Hunger Games*
- *Winter is Coming: Symbols, Portents, and Hidden Meanings in A Game of Thrones*
- *Winning the Game of Thrones: The Host of Characters and their Agendas*
- *Doctor Who: The What Where and How*
- *Sherlock: Every Canon Reference You May Have Missed in BBC's Series 1-3*
- *Women in Game of Thrones: Power, Conformity, and Resistance*

Once a lecturer at San Jose State University, she's a frequent speaker on fantasy, myth, pop culture, and the heroine's journey and can be found at http://vefrankel.com.

SYMBOLS IN GAME OF THRONES

CPSIA information can be obtained at www.ICGtesting.com
Printed in the USA
LVOW08s0018110416

483011LV00001B/97/P